Lincoln Christian College

W9-CBP-846

American Puritanism

Faith and Practice

PILOTBOOKS

DEALING WITH SIGNIFICANT QUESTIONS
FROM THE AMERICAN PAST

Under the Editorship of

Lawrence H. Leder, Lehigh University
Norman K. Risjord, University of Wisconsin
Walter T. K. Nugent, Indiana University

Published in

THE LIPPINCOTT HISTORY SERIES
Under the Editorship of

Robert F. Byrnes, Indiana University
Robert D. Cross, Swarthmore College

American Puritanism

Faith and Practice

by DARRETT B. RUTMAN

UNIVERSITY OF NEW HAMPSHIRE

J. B. LIPPINCOTT COMPANY

Philadelphia
New York
Toronto

Second Printing

Copyright © 1970 by Darrett B. Rutman.
All rights reserved. With the exception of brief excerpts for review,
no part of this book may be reproduced in any form or by any means
without written permission from the publisher.
Library of Congress Catalog Card Number: 79-100370
Printed in the United States of America

FOR BOB BERKHOFER

49970

Preface

The number of books about early America with some form of the word *Puritan* in the title is inordinately large. I myself have already contributed one, *Winthrop's Boston: Portrait of a Puritan Town*, using the adjective almost tongue-in-cheek for I found in early Boston little of the Puritan dominance normally attributed to New England—a fact that critics were quick to resent. Why, then, another book on Puritanism? The explanation might be simply that I was invited to do the book by the editors of this series; but to be invited, while flattering, does not necessarily require acceptance. I accepted because I specifically wanted to address myself to a question: How might the words *Puritan* and *Puritanism* be used in understanding the American past? And I thought that such a question had pertinence within the scope of the series.

In the writing of American history the words *Puritan* and *Puritanism* have generally served to mark something that came to New England in the seventeenth century, gave form to that section, and became a factor in our evolving national society. But the words have been left vague and imprecisely defined. American historians have written of Puritanism as an amorphous, ethereal attitude toward God, life, politics, business, and morality and tended to equate Puritanism with early New England *in toto*. Indeed, some historians have delighted in the absence of precise definition and made a virtue of vagueness. Michael McGiffert, for example, in presenting an excellent survey of contemporary Puritan scholarship to a 1968 conference of early American historians, spoke of the "particular glory of Puritan studies to have maintained, against the temptation to become precisionistic (which is to say, puritanical), a certain accommodating ineffability. . . . Definitional diversity appears to be a sign, and may be a safeguard, of vitality." I cannot agree.

To my mind the vagueness which McGiffert lauds has created confusion in the writing of early American history. It has, on the one hand, given rise to a stream of brilliant, imagistic overviews of a collective "New England mind." On the other, however, this vaguely defined Puritanism has found no place or only an uncomfortable place in the precise, rigorous application of social science methodology which has marked much of the most recent scholarship. In essence two schools of thought have grown up, one devoted to New England as a Puritan *idea*, the other devoted to the study of New England as a *society*, each tending to be oblivious of the other. The present volume attempts to bridge the gap between these schools.

The volume proceeds from several assumptions. First, that while such words as *Puritan* and *Puritanism* might have historic reality in the sense that one man of a specific time and place might refer to another man as Puritan, Puritanism as a historian's concept is an artificial construct, a formulation of reality rather than a reality itself, a part of the framework by which the historian orders his data. Second, that concepts such as Puritanism serve as analytic tools and that as tools they must be sharply defined to be useful. Third, that the historian is free to impart his own definition to a concept, subjecting that definition only to the test of viability: Does the concept so defined contribute to an understanding of the society with which he is concerned? Specifically, I have defined Puritanism in terms of a particular "Christian fellowship" of ministers. Puritanism so defined I conceptualize as but one single element in the complex of elements which gave form to early New England and, insofar as we can extend the influence of New England society, to the American society as a whole.

The work offered is certainly not definitive. In form it is
a series of related essays; in sum it suggests a way of approaching American Puritanism. A full application of that way would
require a book ten times as long and far more complex. Neither
is it an easy book to read. History properly is the description
of the sequential action and interaction of social parts—a cum-
bersome subject. Puritanism as conceptualized here involves
the impact of a religious message upon the mind, and our cum-
bersome subject is made even more so by the necessity of dip-
ping into psychology. The stress upon Puritanism as a historian's concept has dictated a commingling of conceptual
abstractions and empirical data. Finally, the fact that our
Puritanism involves theology creates difficulties. Theology is
an alien subject to most of us in the twentieth century, and
while I have tried to generalize and simplify, I have undoubtedly pleased nobody. Those unaccustomed to theology will
find even simplification and generalization difficult while those
few well versed in the subject will accuse me of doing violence
to it by oversimplifying and overgeneralizing. I can only answer the former by saying that *some* theological consideration
is absolutely necessary, and the latter by pointing to the plight
of the former.

I should add that the ensuing chapters were developed over a
number of years in the process of offering a course on Puritanism as a historical concept at the University of Minnesota, and
thank my former colleagues there for the opportunity to offer
such an offbeat course. Notions basic to the volume were
aired at several sessions during meetings of the American Historical Association and the Organization of American Historians, and before faculty-student groups at the State University of New York at Stony Brook and Buffalo. For their
encouragement and criticism I would like to thank especially
Sidney E. Mead of the University of Iowa, Frederick B. Tolles
of Swarthmore College, Jackson T. Main of the Department
of History and Benjamin Nelson of the Department of Sociology, State University of New York at Stony Brook, Lewis

C. Perry of the State University of New York at Buffalo, B. Katherine Brown of East Lansing, Michigan, and John M. Bumsted of Simon Fraser University. Sydney V. James of the University of Iowa, Kenneth A. Lockridge of the University of Illinois, Chicago Circle, and, of the series editors, Lawrence H. Leder, were kind enough to read and criticize the entire manuscript. While I have not adopted all of their suggestions, the work has been immeasurably improved by virtue of their efforts. It has benefited, too, from the patient encouragement of Alexander K. Fraser, former vice-president and managing editor of the College Department of J. B. Lippincott Company, and the editorial skills of Robert Ritchie, editor.

A synthetic volume such as this—one which encompasses personal research but leans most heavily on the great body of prior work regarding the subject—is, of course, greatly indebted to a vast number of scholars. In my notes and in the brief bibliographical essay appended I have attempted to cite as many as I could by way of thanks. That my approach is more often than not different from that of other commentators on Puritanism does not reduce my debt or my gratitude. I have been privileged, too, to read in manuscript form a number of forthcoming studies which add greatly to an understanding of New England's social history—most notably Professor Lockridge's study of Dedham, Massachusetts, and Philip Greven's of Andover. Needless to say I have received substantial assistance from my graduate students. The dissertation prepared by Robert F. Scholz—" 'The Reverend Elders': Faith, Fellowship, and Politics in the Ministerial Community of Massachusetts Bay, 1630-1710"—has been invaluable, as has the work of Mr. Paul R. Lucas, Mr. Jon M. Butler, Mrs. Leota Keir Hirsch, and Miss Mary Lange. Finally—and by way of elaborating upon the dedication—I must acknowledge my great debt to Robert F. Berkhofer, Jr., now at the University of Wisconsin but my colleague while we both held forth at the University of Minnesota. A self-confessed "generalist," his methodological exegesis while sipping gin and tonic and gazing at the sun setting over Lake Minnetonka set *me* thinking along methodological lines.

D. B. R.

The University of New Hampshire
Durham
June, 1969

Contents

CHAPTER 1

THE CHRISTIAN FELLOWSHIP

Two Puritans

A day early in May, 1628, in the Cornhill ward of London: Robert Keayne, "citizen and merchant tailor of London," settled comfortably into a chair in the home of Matthew Cradock, governor of the New England Company. Carefully Keayne sharpened his quill pen, set an ink bottle beside him, and opened his journal, then waited expectantly for the lecturer to begin. The minister invited to address the Company that day was Master John Cotton of Boston, Lincolnshire, and as Cotton rose to speak, Keayne poised his pen to jot down the text: Isaiah, Chapter 26, verse 20—in the minister's peculiar translation, "Come my children."[1]

The text, Cotton explained, was clear: God would not have his children lost, even in times of greatest danger. And this was assuredly a "comfort to the Godly." In times of peace God might seem "to neglect his children" for "all things fall alike to all." "Yet in the times of public danger and calamity, God will provide and take care of his." Some might object to

---

[1] Robert Keayne's Journal of John Cotton's English Sermons, 1620s, MS in the possession of the Massachusetts Historical Society, Boston. All quotations have been partially modernized.

1

this interpretation, pointing out that "affliction often begins at
God's house and stays at his sanctuary." True! "God may
begin his judgments at the sanctuary," yet he will "take care
to provide for his people, his marked ones"; "he will press and
depress his love to his hidd[en] children," yet it is not the children he is after but the "many hypocrites, loose Christians"
who have entered the sanctuary.

The text, therefore, comforts God's children. It exhorts as
well. If you want God's love and protection, "give yourselves
more to God. Let his law bear sway in you. Give up yourselves with gladness of heart to obey his command and observe
his statutes." "That which terrifies men in evil hours and
hinders the light of God's countenance . . . is guiltiness of the
conscience, when it has gone astray from God's love and command." Moreover, the text "seems to teach God's children, in
all their passions, hates and extremities, not to dishonor the
name of God" for "God is never in such a passion, but he can
hide and save us, and shall we forget God in our hearts and
speak unadvisedly when he never forgets us; shall we deal
worse with God than he deals" with us?

What shall the good children do when the Father vents His
wrath toward the bad? Heed Isaiah! "Behold, thou shalt see
in that day when thou shalt go into an inner chamber to hide
thyself." "My children, get you into your houses! Enter into
your chamber and shut the door after you! Hide yourselves
till wrath be passed over!" Hide in a "private and secret place
to search and examine [thy] heart and ways. Look into your
hearts and there stilly and privately search thoroughly and see
what is in you that might move God to punish you as well as
all the world." But what does this mean? "By entering into
the chamber is signified mewing and sighing and pouring out
our grief for our sins." "By shutting the door after us is
meant shutting out our sins and evils." By hiding ourselves
"is meant our looking up to Christ Jesus for protection and
salvation and preservation—to hide ourselves in Christ by faith."

Oh get you home [to search] into your own hearts. See what evils they be that hang upon you, and whatsoever you see in family, church or commonwealth. And go into your chambers moved for them. Bewail them and leave them not there. But . . . look to God for mercy. Hide yourselves in the covenant and promises of God, and whatsoever evils come, keep thy own souls. Be quiet and all shall be well with you.

Let none delude themselves. God's punishment is "poured out upon the inhabitants of the earth . . . with indignation"; it "is provoked by the indignity and base dealing" of men toward God. "We are," therefore, "worthy" of all that God pours out upon us, "for have not we dealt unworthily with God?" Have we not disdained "his word, ordinances, ministers?"

Did not we deal unworthily with God when we loathed his food and in our hearts waxed weary of it and turned back to Egypt again? When we look upon sanctification and all ways of holiness as upon base and unworthy things? When a man will not be seen publicly to profess religion? When we think it will not stand with our countenance to speak for religion or profess it? Did we not deal unworthily with God when we are so proud that we despise entering into our chambers and searching into our hearts and shutting out sin? Have we not dealt unworthily with God when we looked upon God's blessings and our great deliverance as unworthy things, and so when we look at all kinds of reformation [in the church] and good laws against popery and profaneness as at unworthy things, and think scorn at the purity of God's ordinances and religion?

What is the lesson in all this? To "the state in general": "Take in good part of God's blessings and look not at his ordinances with a disdainful eye; deal not unworthily with God." To "every man in particular": "Learn to deal well with God. Receive his message, Law, spirit! Obey [and] serve him!"

The lecture ended and Keayne closed his journal. Later, perhaps that night, he would open it again for study, casting up in his own mind whether he was dealing well with the Lord, whether he was properly hid in his chamber with the other children of the Lord. But for now there was business to be attended to. He was, after all, a merchant tailor of the city, and the New England Company, in which he had invested one hundred pounds sterling, was a business venture.

WHAT IS PURITANISM? SEVERAL DEFINITIONS AND AN APPROACH

Robert Keayne, citizen and merchant, and John Cotton, minister, are both considered English Puritans; both would eventually journey to what has been labeled Puritan New England, there to live out their lives. But what is the meaning of this word *Puritan?* What does it denote by way of a concept useful in understanding the life, structure, and course of events in early New England?

The word, if it is to be useful to us, is certainly not to be defined as simple religiosity. A useful definition must stipulate the peculiar quality of the thing denoted by the word defined, and religiosity is not peculiar to any single thing of the seventeenth century. Indeed, religiosity pervades the air of that time. In England, men argued and finally fought their Civil War "in the name of God, Amen." Ships sailing from England's ports carried chaplains to pray for the souls of men and the subsiding of God-angried seas. England's expansion overseas was both commanded and justified by God. Thus the English migration to Virginia was that of "a peculiar people, marked and chosen by the finger of God, to possess it, for undoubtedly he is with us."[2] And in English colonies scattered around the Atlantic littoral, prayers were constantly sent heavenward from thousands of throats.

This seventeenth century was an age when all men defined themselves, their society, their activities, and their institutions in terms of God; when the meanest plowboy could feel himself to be, like the sparrow, the immediate object of God's concern; when life itself was considered but a layover on a trip that led to infinity's end. "If it be for his glory," John

---

[2] Virginia's John Rolfe, quoted in Perry Miller, *Errand into the Wilderness* (Cambridge, Mass., 1958), p. 119.

Winthrop wrote to his wife upon leaving England for New England in 1630, God "will bring us together again." If not, "blessed be our God, that we are assured, we shall meet one day, if not as husband and wife, yet in a better condition."[3] And almost seventy years later Virginian William Fitzhugh would write to his mother: "Before I was ten years old, as I am sure you very well remember, I look'd upon this life here as but going to an Inn, no permanent being[.] By God's [will] I continue the same good thoughts and notions still, therefore am always prepared for my certain dissolution."[4] This is, of course, not to say that religion pervaded life and thought to such an extent that one can approach the century by no other avenue but the religious. To pervade is not necessarily to dominate. There are economic, political, and esthetic themes in the seventeenth century as well as religious, and if religion pervades these other themes, it does not follow that it dominates them. When, for example, a given venture is put forth as one

> Whence glory to the name of God, and countries
> good shall spring,
> And unto all that further it, a private gain
> shall bring. . . .[5]

are we to say that the venture is set afoot for purely religious purposes? Religion pervaded seventeenth-century society as an absolute premise, an aspect of life and thought which it was inconceivable to be without, no more and no less.

Puritanism, therefore, is not to be defined simply as religiosity. It must, however, be defined within the context of a pervasive religiosity.

---

[3] Massachusetts Historical Society, *Winthrop Papers* (Boston, 1929-47), II, 225-26.

[4] Richard Beale Davis, ed., *William Fitzhugh and His Chesapeake World, 1676-1701: The Fitzhugh Letters and Other Documents* (Chapel Hill, N.C., 1963), p. 358.

[5] John Hawkins, quoted in Louis B. Wright, *Religion and Empire* (Chapel Hill, N.C., 1943), p. 11.

Neither is Puritanism usefully defined as a peculiar and unique set of social, economic, or political attitudes, although to do so is highly fashionable in some quarters. Two related arguments lie behind such a definition. In the first, England, as the sixteenth century turned to the seventeenth, is conceived to have been in the midst of economic transition as a pastoral, semifeudal system slowly gave way to modern industrial capitalism. Puritanism arose with a creed and ethic to rationalize the activities and aspirations of a new "middle class"—a class midway between lord and peasant which was coming to monopolize capital. Therefore, Puritanism is definable by describing a certain set of middle-class attitudes toward society, economics, and political structure. That set of ideas arrived in America via New England to form the basis of a peculiar American ethic. The second argument is a variant of the first. Again, England is conceived to have been in the midst of transition; flux and change evoked feelings of insecurity in some which in turn evoked a desire to perfect and purify the world within the Christian tradition—perfect and purify the church (thus Puritanism is to be defined as a peculiar religious phenomenon), but also society as a whole (Puritanism defined as a peculiar set of social, political, and economic ideas). Both arguments have application far beyond Puritanism. The same flux and change are seen as pervasive throughout western Europe, evoking either the same rationalization for an emerging middle class or the same desire to perfect and purify. On this larger scale the phenomenon is conceived as the Protestant Reformation and Puritanism as the Reformation "writ small."

Puritanism (and the Reformation) must assuredly be conceived within a complex of change and insecurity. And whatever the words are meant to denote must certainly be conceived within a body of social, economic, and political thought, shaping and being shaped by that body of thought. But it hardly seems useful to define such concepts by describing the flux and insecurity within which they are conceived to be operating or the thought which they are conceived to have provoked. Concepts so defined are invariably overburdened by the infusion of causes and effects, so all-embracing and amorphous as to be useless as analytic tools, and in their tendency to subsume the general within conceptual boundaries pretending to be particular, conducive to sterile controversy.[6]

Finally, Puritanism does not seem usefully defined in geographic terms. No English historian has yet had the audacity to suggest that the people of a given area were English Puritans, hence what those people were and what they thought was English Puritanism. Yet American historians concerned with American Puritanism habitually do just this. "Important as Puritanism has undoubtedly been in shaping the nation," one wrote, "it is more easily described than defined." And it "may perhaps best be described as that point of view, that philosophy of life, that code of values which was carried to New England by the first settlers in the early seventeenth century." The writer was Perry Miller, undoubtedly the most erudite American commentator on Puritanism in the twentieth century.[7] The approach is not without its rationalization.

---

[6] See e.g., Timothy Hall Breen, "The Non-Existent Controversy: Puritan and Anglican Attitudes on Work and Wealth, 1600-1640," *Church History*, XXV (1966), 273-87, and the larger and more general study by Charles and Katherine George, *The Protestant Mind of the English Reformation, 1570-1640* (Princeton, 1961). Basil Hall, "Puritanism: The Problem of Definition," in C. J. Cuming, ed., *Studies in Church History*, II (London, 1965) deals delightfully with the problem of defining English Puritanism, writing (p. 287) that "Puritanism originally a useful coin of some value has become overminted and ended in headlong inflation."

[7] Perry Miller, "Introduction," *in idem* and Thomas H. Johnson, comps., *The Puritans* (rev. ed.; New York, 1963), I, 1. Given the application by others of this broad definition—described *infra*—Miller would undoubtedly agree as to its weakness. A few pages on in this same work he wrote that "Puritanism was a movement toward certain ends within the culture and state of England in the late sixteenth and early seventeenth centuries. . . . It is necessary to belabor the point, because most accounts of Puritanism . . . attribute everything that Puritans said or did to the fact that they were Puritans; their attitudes toward all sorts of things are pounced upon and exhibited as peculiarities of their sect, when as a matter of fact they were normal attitudes for the time." Still later he stipulated that what was found in New England was one-tenth Puritanism and nine-tenths mere "Englishism." Unfortunately, he neither elaborated nor stipulated a definition by which the one-tenth could be discerned from the nine-tenths.

Throughout the seventeenth century New England's leaders proclaimed their society to be Puritan and unique. But one can suggest that the definition is inadequate for our purposes. In order to explore the workings of whatever we define as Puritanism in the forming of New England—even in forming this persistent self-identification of New England leaders—we must first separate Puritanism *from* New England.

Certainly the definition of Puritanism by description of New England leads to awkward assumptions. If, for example, Puritanism cannot be explicitly defined, only described as a point of view carried to New England in the early seventeenth century, then one easily assumes that what one finds in early New England is Puritanism. And inasmuch as Puritanism is implicitly unique—else why use such a qualitative word at all?—what one finds in New England is by implication unique. New England is marked by religiosity; religiosity is therefore a mark of Puritanism and is unique to New England. But of course we have already noted that religiosity is pervasive in the century, to be found in New England and old, in old England and Virginia. The data, consequently, do not fit. Or to choose another example: The custom of parents putting their children out to work as servants in other families is found in New England; it is, therefore, a Puritan trait rationalized in Puritan terms—the Puritan felt that children were degenerate until they underwent godly conversion and put them out to other families so that parental love would not vitiate the discipline required toward the degenerate. Yet the custom of putting children out to serve in other families was not peculiar but customary in the traditional England from which Puritanism emerged.[8]

Moreover, American Puritanism, approached in this way, is a single entity—"*that* point of view, *that* philosophy . . . *that* code." The implication is that there was a single "unity" running "in Puritan thought, expression, and mannners."[9] Given

---

[8] Edmund S. Morgan, *The Puritan Family: Religion and Domestic Relations in Seventeenth-Century New England* (new ed., rev. and enlarged; New York, 1966), pp. 75 ff. *Cf. infra*, chap. II.

[9] Miller and Johnson, comps., *The Puritans*, I, v.

this, and given the tendency to equate Puritanism and early New England, it follows that one can assume an absolute unity in early New England, that one can talk of the early New Englanders monolithically. In other words, if one finds among one group of New Englanders a given idea, that idea is a Puritan idea, therefore a New England idea, therefore an idea held by all New Englanders. One example suffices: an excellent study of the doctrine of preparation as held by New England ministers which begins, *"Seventeenth-century New Englanders* examined their hearts with an intensity now quite alien to the American mind."[10] The assumption of a monolithic New England is undoubtedly serviceable to historians of the later colonial years who address themselves to the transition from "Puritan to Yankee." One can write trenchantly of the disintegration of Puritan New England, of the "decline of the animating ideal of a whole society." And the stereotype Puritan New England of the early years is a marvelous contrast against which one can display the vibrant Yankeeism of the later.[11] But the close study of the structure of life—a mark of the most recent scholarly excursions into the seventeenth century—is ill-served by a definition of Puritanism in which is inherent the notion of a New England monolith. Data cannot be made to conform. The monolith, as such studies are showing, simply did not exist.[12]

[10] Norman Pettit, *The Heart Prepared: Grace and Conversion in Puritan Spiritual Life* (New Haven and London, 1966), p. 1. Italics inserted.

[11] John M. Murrin, "Anglicizing an American Colony: The Transformation of Provincial Massachusetts" (unpublished Ph.D. dissertation, Yale University, 1966), p. 27. The "Puritan to Yankee" theme is common. Note simply titles: Richard L. Bushman, *From Puritan to Yankee: Character and the Social Order in Connecticut, 1690-1765* (Cambridge, Mass., 1967); Richard S. Dunn, *Puritans and Yankees: The Winthrop Dynasty of New England, 1630-1717* (Princeton, 1962).

[12] For a preliminary assessment see my "The Mirror of Puritan Authority" in George A. Billias, ed., *Law and Authority in Colonial America* (Barre, Mass., 1965); the introduction to Sydney V. James, ed., *The New England Puritans* (New York, 1968); J. M. Bumsted and J. T. Lemon, "New Approaches in Early American Studies: The Local Community in New England," *Histoire Sociale/Social History*, II (1968), 98-112.

If not in terms of religiosity per se, peculiar and unique social notions, or the people of a particular area, how are we to conceptualize Puritanism in such a way that we can use the concept in understanding the society of early New England and, to an extent, American society as a whole? The scene with which this chapter opened—that of layman Robert Keayne listening to minister John Cotton and jotting down the main points of the sermon for future study—suggests what might be a useful approach. Assuming both men to be Puritans, Puritanism can be conceived as something imparted by ministers such as Cotton to laymen such as Keayne. Our focus is immediately upon ministers as the givers of this gift of Puritanism.

The English Reformation and the Beginnings of a Distinction

English Puritanism, if we are to judge by those ministers who have come down to us with the label Puritan, was certainly a religious phenomenon which stressed the sovereignty of God, the paramountcy of the Bible in revealing the will of God, and the absolute necessity of men's subsuming themselves to God. To the Puritan minister, the central point of man's history was the Adamic legend—the sin and subsequent expulsion of God's first couple from the Garden. Man's purpose was the attempt to regain the Garden, at least in a spiritual, other-worldly sense. The process of regaining the Garden was understood to be beyond the ability of mere man, debased and degenerate as he was, for God, for his own purposes, through Christ, had himself elected and redeemed a given number of men. But the Puritan minister nevertheless insisted that men work and strive, some vainly, some successfully.

In none of this, however, did the Puritan minister deviate from the creedal basis of England's early reformed church establishment. In the 1530s, Henry VIII had removed England from the jurisdiction of the Pope in Rome and cautiously, ambiguously, aligned the realm with the continental Reforma-

tion. Reformation notions had seeped into England, commingling with indigenous English notions about the nature and
interrelationship of God, Christ, the church, and man. During
the reign of Edward VI (1547-53) the new ideas had poured
into the realm to be officially promulgated as the articles of
England's faith. The reign of Catholic Mary had reversed
the tide, but Elizabeth's accession in 1558 recommitted England to reformed doctrine, and the Edwardian articles of faith
were reiterated with slight amendment:

> There is but one living and true God everlasting, without
> body, parts, or passions; of infinite power, wisdom, and good-
> ness; the Maker and Preserver of all things.
>
> It is the fault and corruption of every man, that naturally is
> engendered of the off-spring of Adam, whereby man is very
> far gone from original righteousness, and is of his own nature
> inclined to evil; so that the flesh lusteth always contrary to the
> spirit; and therefore in every person born into this world it
> deserveth God's wrath and damnation.
>
> In the Old Testament, as in the New, everlasting life is offered
> to mankind by Christ, who is the only Mediator betwixt God
> and man, being both God and man.
>
> Christ in the truth of our nature was made like unto us in all
> things (sin only excepted) from which he was clearly void
> both in his flesh and in his spirit: he came to be a lamb with-
> out spot, who by sacrifice of himself once made should take
> away the sins of the world: . . . but all we the rest (although
> baptized and born in Christ) yet offend.
>
> Predestination unto life, is the everlasting purpose of God
> whereby (before the foundations of the world were laid) he
> hath constantly decreed by his counsel, secret unto us, to de-
> liver from curse and damnation those whom he hath chosen in
> Christ out of mankind, and to bring them by Christ to ever-
> lasting salvation.[13]

If there was no Puritan deviation from this established
dogma—early or late—there was from the very beginning devi-

---

[13] Gilbert Burnet, *The History of the Reformation of the Church of
England* (Oxford, 1865), V, 314 ff. quoting Articles I, VI, VIII, XIV, and
XVII of 1552 and 1562.

ation from the spirit of the establishment. Dogma was the creation of intellectuals—the scholars of the universites, Cambridge and Oxford, the archbishops, bishops, "and other learned men." It was sealed by monarchs and statesmen. And it was purveyed to the generality of England, much diluted, in the *Book of Common Prayer* and in homilies approved by the hierarchy and appointed by the state to be read before all the congregations of England, homilies "against peril of idolatry," "against gluttony and drunkenness," "against idleness." But there were particular ministers—even as dogma was being promulgated—who were intellectuals in that they were products of Cambridge and Oxford but evangelists as well, men who took literally the biblical injunction, "Go ye therefore and teach." The world, they cried, was ignorant of God; they must, therefore, take dogma (pure truth) and the Bible (the proof of truth) into the fields and marketplaces to spread Christian enlightenment, impart Christian responsibility, and dispel superstition.

Dogma, moreover, was to such ministers veneered upon what they considered an imperfectly reformed church. Ritualism and an episcopal structure of archbishops, bishops, and archdeacons, ecclesiastical courts and commissions—ritualism and an episcopacy little changed from Catholic days—remained. To these ministers, however, the church was simply "God's schoolhouse."[14] At best, ritualism and episcopacy were "inconsequential" to the primary work of educating all men to a Christian way; at worst, when such things worked against educating men, they were anathema. The essence of the pure religious condition was the individual's confrontation with God and with God's will; peripheral but essential were the minister —teaching, exhorting, and guiding the individual—and the gathering together of individuals, that they might help and encourage each other. What help in this situation was the ritual use of the sign of the cross, the kneeling for communion

14 Patrick Collinson, *The Elizabethan Puritan Movement* (Berkeley and Los Angeles, 1967), p. 173, quoting Thomas Cooper, Bishop of Lincoln.

as prescribed by the established service, the wearing of special vestments by the minister? What help was the episcopal structure which set a hierarchy over the minister? Indeed, was not ceremony truly a pernicious thing, tending to distract the Christian from the primary goal—his confrontation with God? Was not the structure antipathetical when it demanded more of religion than simple education or when it stood in the way of education? And what a hindrance were the prayers and litanies set down in the *Book of Common Prayer*, the homilies! Ministers constrained to such formalities and banalities could hardly speak appropriately to the condition of their hearers. The denunciation by such ministers as we have been describing of these elements of the English establishment led many at the time to consider them as merely desiring a purification—hence the word Puritan was coined—and they are frequently described in terms of what they were against. What is most pertinent, however, is what they stood for: the intense and evangelical advocacy of the Christian obligation to know and serve God.

Ardent Preachers and a Christian Fellowship

Let us name some of these ministers. There was Richard Greenham, a humble, gentle man, a student at Cambridge in the 1560s (when the Edwardian articles were being reiterated) and for twenty years after 1570 rector of Dry Drayton parish near Cambridge. Arthur Hildersham was another. The son of Catholic parents, he eschewed the old faith for the new and, after studying at Cambridge, ministered first to the parish of Ashby-de-la-Zouch, later as an itinerant lecturer in Leicestershire. Still a third was John Dod. His was a long career of preaching begun when he left Cambridge in 1585. For almost twenty years he ministered at Hanwell, Oxfordshire. Silenced by order of his bishop for nonconformity in 1604, he moved to Warwick, then to Northampton, where in 1645— well over ninety years of age—he was to die. Laurence Chaderton, for fifty years lecturer at St. Clement's Church,

Cambridge, and for almost forty years master of Emmanuel College, was a fourth. Still another was Richard Rogers, long-time "Preacher of God's Word" in and around the village of Wethersfield, Essex. There were others, but these are an exemplifying five. They were masters in the art of the care of souls.

The care—or, in a broad rather than technical sense, the "cure"—of souls! Here was the key. To dispel superstition, spread Christian enlightenment, and impart Christian responsibility—acts prompted by the evangelical zeal—was to leave men floundering. Made conscious of particular sin, men sought relief from conscience; made conscious of their innately sinful nature, they sought answer to the fundamental question: "What can I do to be saved?" Polemicists arguing over vestments or the episcopacy, collegiates probing dead languages that they might add an iota to the meaning of a biblical phrase —both were too busy to help, the first with their arguments, the second with their conceits. Thus Greenham complained that the polemicists "help little to godliness, but rather fill the heads and hearts of men with a spirit of contradiction and contention." The truth "might lie on either side, or on neither." The discourses of Cambridge scholars he dismissed as "so cold and so human, that the simple preaching of Christ doth greatly decay." "They whose knowledge is in swelling words and painted eloquence of human wisdom . . . preach and delight to hear plausible novelties, to please the ear rather than the simple power of the word to pierce the heart."[15] Neither could the usual parish priest help. Some ostentatiously displayed their learning in Latin, Greek, and Hebrew which, of course, their listeners could not comprehend. Others turned their pulpits into playhouses, telling "fond fables to make their hearers laugh." And still others were incapable of preaching at all—the uneducated and obviously degenerate Parson Levitt,

---

[15] Quoted in William Haller, *The Rise of Puritanism* (New York, 1938), pp. 26-27; Samuel Clarke, ed., *A General Martyrologie . . . Whereunto Is Added the Lives of Thirty Two English Divines* (London, 1677), p. 13.

for example, "a notorious swearer, a dicer, a carder, a hawker and hunter, a very careless person" who "had a child by a maid since he was instituted and inducted." Perhaps he mouthed a homily once in a while, but more likely he exemplified Anthony Gilby's soldier-turned-cleric who "read a hasty service and then went merrily to one's dinner, without any foolishness such as instructing the common people."[16]

Such men as Greenham, Hildersham, Dod, Chaderton, and Rogers, however, learned and exemplary in their own lives, shouldered the burden of their parishioners as their own. They were strenuous and articulate preachers, constantly exhorting their flocks to self-examination and self-assessment. "Where do you stand with God today?" they asked. But they also gave their listeners a gauge by which to answer.

The preachers' doctrine can be summed up in five words: election, vocation, justification, sanctification, glorification. An absolute God freely and graciously elects those he will save (election); but he also calls those he elects (vocation); and those he calls feel faith in Christ building within them, their sins are remitted, and the righteousness of Christ is imputed to them (justification); justification emboldens and hardens them in their battles with the sin of the world and their own flesh (sanctification); and so hardened they live a life that merits, although it does not earn, salvation (glorification). Fatalism and antinomianism were the horns of the dilemma posed by such a doctrine: If God graciously elects, there is nothing the individual can or should do with regard to his own spiritual condition; or, if one is of the elect, he is superior to all law and morality, for he is as a transformed creature, a God-man. Both horns were avoided by the preachers as they accented the necessity of preparation and the quest for assurance as to God's promise of salvation for the elect. Men could not merely sit back and await God's pleasure but were obliged to attend to the ministry of the Word, seek under-

---

[16] Edmund S. Morgan, *Visible Saints: The History of a Puritan Idea* (New York, 1963), pp. 7-8; M. M. Knappen, *Tudor Puritanism: A Chapter in the History of Idealism* (Chicago, 1939), p. 200.

standing of what is good and what evil, appreciate their own
"peculiar and proper sins," convince themselves of their help-
less and hopeless condition. Nor could they too facilely seize
upon assurance of their salvation—that was the way of hypocrites. Assurance came agonizingly slowly as the elect responded to God's irresistible call; its progress had to be measured and studied, doubted and tested. Logically, preparation
and assurance were separate, the former an obligation on all
men, the latter involving the elect alone. But the two were
regularly slurred together to form a single, elaborate morphology of conversion, a structured series of steps from the first
realization of God's Word (the Bible) to the final quaking,
tremulous hopefulness. All men were urged to start the climb,
and the fact that only a few were predestined to reach the
top was more often than not lost sight of by both preachers
and listeners: Let no man "presently conclude that he is a
reprobate: but let him rather use the word of God, and the
sacraments, that he may have an inward sense of the power of
Christ, drawing him unto him," one preacher wrote.[17]

The preachers were patient physicians of the soul involved
in this tedious, all-important climb. Having established in their
sermons the necessity for and the various steps in preparation
and assurance, they guided their parishioners along the way,
counselling those troubled by quandaries and doubts. Master
Dod was habitually in his church, and those coming to him
with questions he would meet "and say, Would you speak
with me? And when he found them unable to state their
question, he would help them out with it, taking care to find
the sore: But would answer and deal so compassionately and
tenderly, as not to discourage the poorest soul from coming
again to him." And of Greenham, a near-contemporary wrote:
"His masterpiece was in comforting wounded consciences. For,
although Heaven's hand can only set a broken heart, yet God

---

[17] *The Workes of that Famous Minister of Christ . . . Mr. William
Perkins* (Cambridge, Eng., 1616-18), I, 113. See also Morgan, *Visible Saints*,
pp. 67 ff.

used him herein as an instrument of good to many, who came to him with weeping eyes, and went from him with cheerful souls."[18]

Such men as we have named were themselves the products of a preaching tradition—one old in England but vastly encouraged during the Protestant infusion of the mid-sixteenth century when, for example, Thomas Becon wrote that his only work in life was "to teach the people."[19] But they crystallized and carried along that tradition. Their fame attracted young students from the universities, particularly Cambridge, first to their sermons where, typically, the student's own religious conscience would be awakened and he would set off along his own path of preparation and assurance. Ultimately the student would find his way to the master's house, where the elder instructed the younger—not so much in classics, oratory, or even to any great extent theology (there was enough instruction in all three at the universities)—but in this art of preaching and the care of souls. The student, for his part, would move out into the ministry to make a reputation for himself, attract new students, and so spread the notion of what a true minister of the Word ought to be. Indeed, the generation of ministers of this sort approaches something of the quality of the opening chapters of Chronicles: Richard Rogers begat (in a spiritual sense) Paul Baynes, who begat Richard Sibbes, who begat John Cotton, who begat John Preston, who begat Thomas Shepard. Chaderton, when he resigned St. Clement's pulpit, was acknowledged by forty ministers as the man who converted them. Master John Wilson —he would sail for New England in 1630—is not untypical. Chaderton's Cambridge sermons "enlightened, and awakened [him] unto more solicitous inquiries after 'the one thing yet lacking in him.' "

---

[18] Clarke, ed., *General Martyrologie*, p. 177; Thomas Fuller, *The Church History of Britain; from the Birth of Jesus Christ Until the Year MDCXLVIII*, J. S. Brewer, ed. (Oxford, 1845), V, 192.

[19] Quoted in A. G. Dickens, *The English Reformation* (London, 1964), p. 225.

Nevertheless, being forestalled with prejudices against the Puritans of those times, as if they had held he knew not well what *odd things,* he declined their acquaintance. . . . Until going to a bookseller's shop, to augment his well-furnished library, he lighted upon that famous book of Mr. Richard Rogers', called 'The *Seven Treatises;*' which when he had read, he so affected, not only the matter, but also the author of the book, that he took a journey unto Wethersfield, on purpose to hear a sermon from that Boanerges. When he had heard the heavenly passages that fell from the lips of that worthy man, privately as well as publicly, and compared therewithal the writings of Greenham, of Dod, and of Dent . . . he saw that they who were nicknamed Puritans, were like to be the desirablest companions for one that intended his own everlasting happiness.[20]

In the end, a Christian fellowship of like-minded ministers and of no small importance was created.

A FELLOWSHIP AT ODDS WITH SOCIETY

In many ways this Christian fellowship was an amorphous continuation of university friendships, its religious overtones merely a reflection of the fact that university men more often than not ended in the ministry. John Knewstubb, rector of Cockfield, visiting his Cambridge schoolfriend Richard Rogers at Wethersfield, would talk of old times, but both being ardent Puritan ministers, they would have "very comfortable and profitable companyings in prayer and conference together" as well.[21] Yet it was more than this.

The evangelical university man, intent on taking truth and the Bible to the generality, was at variance with his society. In a general way it was implicit in the situation. What need was there for his strident evangelicalism if the world about him (as he viewed it) was not ignorant and sinful, mindful of this world's goods at the expense of the next world's blessings, prone to snicker at Shakespeare's bawds and frequent Sabbath

---

[20] Cotton Mather, *Magnalia Christi Americana; or, The Ecclesiastical History of New England* (Hartford, 1852-53), I, 303-04.

[21] M. M. Knappen, ed., *Two Elizabethan Puritan Diaries* (Chicago, 1933), p. 95.

gatherings at the tavern rather than church. If the world had been as the Puritan minister would have it, there would have been no Puritan minister.

A more particular variance was a greater cross, however. What the preacher considered inconsequential or antipathetical to his role as teacher and exhorter, although commanded of him by church hierarchy and crown, he tended to dispense with, becoming a "non-conformist" in a society which valued conformity. And what he stressed—the sermon, popular edification—the hierarchy and crown tended to de-emphasize. Elizabeth, in her cautious way, attempted to curb sermonizing; a good homily on obedience was enough! James I, in 1604, complained of those who "placeth all religion in the ear, through which there is an easy passage." (In his native Scotland he had been more direct, shouting at a minister, "I give not a turd for your preaching.")[22]

Moreover, the intellectual temper was changing, increasing the Puritan preacher's variance. The original creedal basis of England's church, which formed the basis of the preacher's doctrine, had been laid down at the height of the Reformation, when the works of Luther, Calvin, Zwingli, Beza, Peter Martyr, Melanchthon had been brunted about in crude but pristine form—cold, harsh sunlight in the winter of decayed Catholicism. Winter had passed, however, and a warm, mellow sun was rising, presaged at Cambridge in the 1590s by theological disputes.[23] The details need not concern us, only the intellectual tempering of the creed which in time found its way into the hierarchy and the churches as an accenting of man's will to the denigration of God's sovereignty, the elevation of nature and reason as sources of divine truth, and an infusion of more and more formalism and ceremonialism, even an imputation that forms and ceremonies were efficacious in

[22] Christopher Hill, *Society and Puritanism in Pre-Revolutionary England* (2d ed.; New York, 1967), p. 63; David H. Willson, *King James VI and I* (New York and London, 1956), p. 71.

[23] H. C. Porter, *Reformation and Reaction in Tudor Cambridge* (Cambridge, Eng. 1958), chap. XVII.

the work of salvation. It was not that the new intellectuals were necessarily less concerned with the pastoral role—indeed, Lancelot Andrewes, a representative of the new, has been coupled with Greenham as a master of the cure of souls. It was that the Puritan preacher, clinging to the old creed, would enlighten man about an omnipotent God and thrust on him the dialectic of salvation (election, vocation, justification, sanctification, and glorification) while the emerging "Anglican" would thrust on man damnation for his sins and salvation by repentance and reformation of his earthly life.

At variance with his society, the Puritan minister tended to cling to his fellows. In the late 1500s, the command of crown and hierarchy to conform and the official de-emphasis of sermons and edification was such as to inspire an effort to overturn the hierarchy and transfer affairs of the church to the godly preachers assembled in conference or classis. The movement, brilliantly described by historian Patrick Collinson, failed.[24] But it left in its wake an inchoate opposition to episcopacy and support for what was discerned in the New Testament as a more legitimate church polity than that established, one that would place more authority in the congregation and its officers and less in bishops. And it left a tradition of ministerial association, together with a literature, biblically based, rationalizing the very idea of association or fellowship.

In the increasingly hostile world of the seventeenth century the fellowship took on an even more vital position in the life of some ministers. Driven into continuing nonconformity, into breaking the unity of the social fabric which, in prevailing thought, was inherently good, one minister sought resolution with others of his kind, reviving the air of unity dispelled by his nonconformity—unity in truth if not within the established order. Such ministers in any given geographic area would gather fairly regularly to discuss common problems and knotty places in Scripture, to observe common fasts and prayerful sessions for "the lamentable evils of the times."[25] When one

---

[24] In his *Elizabethan Puritan Movement,* cited *supra.*
[25] Benjamin Brook, *The Lives of the Puritans* (London, 1813), II, 44.

of their leading figures died, they would arrange for the collecting, editing, and publishing of his sermons and assign to one of their number the writing of a commendatory biography. And when a young minister appeared in their midst and they were assured of his soundness, they would solicit a position for him. The publication of tracts and sermons and occasional travels of the members—to London particularly, and to the commencement exercises at the universities—kept such local groups in touch with others to give a roughly national configuration to the fellowship. In all of this, however, the ministers acted informally, ambiguously. Their union was less institutional and more natural, the amorphous companionship of old friends and fellow workers. If they acknowledged this or that voice among them as superior it was on the basis of ability in performing God's work, on reputation—no more. And if they acknowledged the corporate authority of the fellowship in even a vague way, their acknowledgement was completely voluntary.

THE ELABORATION OF THE DISTINCTION

In the beginning—in the sixteenth century—the Puritan minister had little more to do than preach and counsel. He was faced with what he termed the superstition of Catholicism on the one hand and ignorance and "dumbness" toward the Christian quest on the other. But, as he worked, the preacher soon faced a threefold rather than twofold division of the .populace: the superstitious, the dumb, and the ardent, educated Christians whom the preacher had awakened to the quest. All three were encompassed in one single, national church establishment. All three solicited the fellowship of the church, the baptism of children, and communion. Was such a commingling desirable? That all should hear the word of God as pronounced by the preachers was certainly justifiable, for it was through the preachers that men were awakened to their obligation. But once awakened, questing Christians needed the fellowship of other equally questing Christians to help them on their way. Frail and weak, they needed the discipline of the group.

So much on a practical level. On a theoretical level the ministers—ardent students of the Bible and of the fathers of the primitive church—asked themselves what constituted a true church. In the rhetoric of the time the one and true church of which Christ was the head consisted of those from among the mass of men for whom Christ had won justification—the elect. Yet the number of elect were few, and the decree of election "secret from us." It followed, therefore, that the true church was "invisible," a gathering of the saints dead, living, and still unborn, existing outside of time. But men and women had gathered in "visible" churches from the time of Christ. The Epistles of the New Testament described the activities of these first churches, and to men who accepted the Bible as a decree from God, it was patently obvious that the continuation of such visible churches was commanded. The theoretical and practical levels conjoined. Was it not proper that the visible church, a creation of man, approximate as closely as possible the invisible church of Christ? And if such were admitted, did it not follow that the ardent, questing Christians—among whom were undoubtedly the greater number of invisible saints—logically constituted a more proper visible church than the commingled mass of all Englishmen? And such questions became intertwined with questions of polity provoked by the inchoate opposition to episcopacy of the late 1500s. What was the proper form of the true visible church? If an episcopal structure was erroneous, what of the ordination of a minister at the hands of a bishop? How was a man called to the ministry of God's world? To be a pastor, teacher, or elder of a particular flock? How was one particular church to commune with another if not through the diocesan office?

These were not easy questions. Some followed logic to its conclusion: The mixture of godly and ungodly damned the entire English establishment. An unwarranted episcopal structure doubly damned it. Hence the godly must withdraw from the establishment and set themselves up as independent, visible churches, governing and disciplining themselves, calling to their service their own proper officers. Apart from the officers of a particular church, there was no ministry—ordination was a sham. Such godly congregations might have voluntary communion with one another, as had the churches of the Epistles, but each particular church was an entity in and of itself. This was separatism, and was at times followed by an abandonment of England entirely—a physical departure from the kingdom such as that which took the future "Pilgrims" from Scrooby to Leyden in the Netherlands. It was an extreme step, however, given the accent on social unity, and few took it, preferring instead any one of a number of halfway positions.

The vast majority of preachers did not abandon England either figuratively or literally as a land of sin and reprobation. On the contrary, they made a fetish of the kingdom, and here Puritanism and nationalism came together. England was a New Israel, a holy people favored of God. The preachers were bitterly critical. Like the biblical Jeremiah they bemoaned the fallen state of the people and the leadership of the bishops—"pastors" who had abandoned their flocks for false riches and empty honors. Indeed, they considered England's sin all the greater because, held so high in the esteem of the Maker, her fall was much the farther than that of any other nation. They called on Englishmen to give up their vanities and conceits and games, commanded them to reform their persons and their institutions (notably the church), and, as the seventeenth century proceeded and men did not, threatened in ever more vigorous terms the coming wrath of the Lord:

> I have seen thine adulteries and thy neighings,
> the lewdness of thy whoredom, and thine abo-
> minations on the hills in the fields. Woe unto thee,
> O Jerusalem![26]

Woe unto thee, O England!
But they did not condemn absolutely. So long as there were

---

[26] Jeremiah 13:27.

sincere, edifying preachers (like themselves) there was hope that all England could be reformed and, in repentance, keep the favor of the Lord.

Neither did any but an infinitesimal minority of the preachers abandon the English religious establishment. True, it was imperfect, but not so imperfect as to prevent the Lord's work from being done, as the separatist held. In their parishes or, in the case of lecturers without formal pastoral charges, in their discourses, the ministers could still preach and awaken men. Many accepted the mixture of godly and ungodly and in a variety of ways found warrant for their acceptance. But a few here and there gathered together the ardent Christians from among their listeners in informal religious fellowship. Thus in Richard Rogers' parish, in the evening after public (and mixed) services, there "met privately" to confer and "edify" each other a part of "that company which came by course that day." Minister John Eliot wrote of his "company of Christians who held frequent communion together." Such fellowships were carried a step toward more formal organizations as some preachers introduced covenants into the meetings, those gathering agreeing to forsake worldly things, to "turn to the Lord in all sincerity," to bind themselves to a common rule, admonish each other's failings, and to make a continuing habit of conferring together by way of forwarding their Christian estate. Still another step was taken when a few preachers began idealizing their gatherings as the proper visible church. This was verging on separatism, yet the line was not overshot. The gathering was an entity separate from but contained within the establishment. John Cotton remained a minister to his entire parish, ordained and sanctioned by his bishop, but he considered the covenanted group he gathered in 1615 the "essential" church, its members, all questing Christians, bound together "in nearer fellowship with God and one another." And the gathering was not, as the separatists tended to hold, a proper visible church only insofar as its forms were pure. Form was not the essence of the pure church to a Cotton—not covenant, not officers, not discipline

—but only the power of God which led men to associate in this manner.[27]

That the preachers should seize upon the covenant in any fashion was only natural. The notion of covenant underlay the social fabric of the time. Men gathered in guilds, in companies, in communities, and in their allegiance to the monarch under the explicit terms of covenants, contracting to give faithful support to the whole in return for the protection and fulfillment of the part. It was also a part of the systematic theology of the Reformation, describing the relationship of man and God. In this latter sense, one wrote of several covenants. By a covenant of works God established a moral law— in its simplest form the Commandments—which all men were obliged to attempt to follow. By a covenant of grace God contracted, through Christ, to bring to salvation those whom Christ's death justified; man was obliged to have faith alone, although axiomatically only the elect could have the true, saving faith which met the condition of the contract.

Covenanted gatherings of questing Christians and covenants within a theological system threw into question the very nature of the sacraments. Moving slowly toward asserting the gatherings to be the proper visible church, the preachers were presented with a quandary: The sacraments were historically central to the notion of the visible church, yet they were dispensed within the mixed parish, remaining in effect the prerogative of the established order. One way out of the dilemma was to consider that while the sacraments were dispensed to all and sundry, they were efficacious only so far as the religious condition of the recipient allowed. By this

---

[27] Richard Rogers, *Seven Treatises, Containing Such Direction as . . . May Be Called the Practise of Christianitie* (London, 1603), pp. 497-98; Knappen, ed., *Two Elizabethan Puritan Diaries*, pp. 67-68; John Eliot to Richard Baxter, October 7, 1657, in F. J. Powicke, ed., *Some Unpublished Correspondence of the Reverend Richard Baxter and the Reverend John Eliot* (Manchester, 1931), pp. 24-25; John Cotton, *The Way of the Congregational Churches Cleared* (London, 1648), p. 20; John Cotton to Samuel Skelton, October 2, 1630, in Thaddeus M. Harris, *Memorials of the First Church in Dorchester* (Boston, 1830), pp. 53-57.

reasoning the recipients from within the gatherings truly received the sacraments; those outside the gatherings received at most a questionable benefit. Covenant theology, however, as theologian Jens G. Møller has pointed out, tended to question the very efficacy of the sacraments themselves.

> If God's elect only attain unto salvation through participation in God's Covenant of Grace . . . what purpose do the sacraments then ultimately serve? Or if the covenant means a mutual contract between God and man with reciprocal conditions . . . then the sacraments signify, more than anything, that through participation in the ordinances the [elect] believer binds himself to obedience in the service of God. But in this latter case the obligation and not the sacrament is what finally counts.[28]

The upshot in either case was that, among the preachers of the fellowship—who, it should be added, accented covenant theology more than any in England—some tended to slight the sacraments. If the essence of the church was in the voluntary gathering and the sacraments in the established churches, what else could they do? And if the essence of salvation was in election, defined in terms of the covenant of grace, the sacraments could hardly be helps along the way to salvation; they could be no more than "seals" of the covenant, God's signature, so to speak, to a bargain made and already met with regard to the elect.

THE GIFT OF THE PREACHERS

But we have come as far as we need along these lines. What we have done, of course, is to sketch a definition of Puritanism as it gradually took form over time to roughly 1630. We started with evangelicalism among a few Cambridge- and Oxford-trained ministers and added elements as the evangelical ministers were confronted by new situations and responded: disdain of unedifying forms and ceremonies, homilies and the like; a theological dialectic (election, vocation, justification,

---

28 Jens G. Møller, "The Beginnings of Puritan Covenant Theology," *Journal of Ecclesiastical History*, XIV (1963), 63.

sanctification, glorification) which, while the common property of English intellectuals at the beginning of Elizabeth's
reign, was more and more exclusively the property of the
Puritan ministers as time progressed and as a tempered doctrine appeared; a doubt as to the legitimacy of an episcopal
hierarchy which, on the one hand, insisted on forms and ceremonies (more often than not at the command of the crown
in the early years), and, on the other, was tending toward that
self-same tempered doctrine; a tradition of voluntary fellowship among the preachers; an assertion of an alternative polity
which would give some or all authority (there were different
claims) to the confreres of the fellowship; and finally, an assertion of varying degrees of positiveness that in the gathering of
questing Christians was to be found the proper visible church.

Notably, we have been concerned only with ministers of the
Gospel. And this has been with intent. Accepting as symbolic the scene of layman Keayne listening avidly to minister
Cotton, we are conceptualizing Puritanism as a gift imparted
by the preachers of the fellowship to the laymen who heard
them preaching. We have ignored, for the moment, the condition of the laymen—the fact that they were perhaps prepared
for the gift by a swirling complex of lay beliefs and doubts
which, in England, one begins to sense in the late fifteenth
and early sixteenth centuries and which swells with the advent
of the Reformation. We have ignored, too, the probability
that the preachers were responding to the needs of their
hearers as evoked by this complex of beliefs and doubts, and
to their own needs as well. Our immediate purpose has been
to establish a clear and precise definition of the gift, and that
purpose has seemed best achieved by eschewing the circumstances of the giving and receiving and looking single-mindedly
at the gift while in the hands of the giver.

Our conceptualization of Puritanism as a gift from the
preachers to their hearers is, as all conceptualizations are, artificial. And like other conceptualizations of Puritanism, it leads
to definition by description. But it has the merit of holding
Puritanism within sharp limitations. Our Puritanism does not

sprawl all over the ideological landscape. It has, moreover, one central element—the evangelical zeal of the ministers expressed within the theological dialectic. Those aspects conjoined with the evangelical zeal as the zealous were confronted with opposition and as unanticipated problems arose to confront them out of their very successes as evangelists are merely peripheral. The conceptualization is not without complications, as we shall see in shifting our attention from the ministers to the laity in an effort to assess the effect of the gift upon the recipients. But perhaps it will prove a viable tool in our ultimate intention of understanding early New England. That remains to be seen.

CHAPTER 2

CHILDREN OF THE FELLOWSHIP

RECIPIENTS OF THE PREACHERS' GIFT

That Master Cotton and Robert Keayne were on hand at the May meeting of the New England Company in 1628—the one, a member of the ministerial fellowship, to lecture, the other, a lay follower of the fellowship, to jot down the main points of the lecture—was not merely fortuitous. Nothing is clearer than the association of the fellowship with first the company and subsequently the great venture into Massachusetts Bay which proceeded from it.

The company had been founded as a result of the activities of Master John White of Dorchester; it numbered among its earliest investors Master Hugh Peter, lecturer at St. Sepulchre's, London; only a few days before Cotton addressed the assembled members, Master Nathaniel Ward, curate of St. James, London, and soon to be rector of Stondon Massey, Essex, had spoken; Masters White and John Davenport of London selected the ministers who would journey to New England in 1629 to serve the religious needs of the settlement—Samuel Skelton of Sempringham, Lincolnshire; Francis Higginson, a lecturing nonconformist from Leicestershire; Francis Bright, a young protegé of Davenport. All of these were ministers of the fellowship. Indeed, in 1629 Master White would address "many reverend Divines" at the Cambridge commencement—a traditional annual gathering of the fellowship—issuing there "a call" for New England. And to read the roster of lay investors in the company is to read one after another the names of prominent lay followers of Puritan ministers.

Yet the initial motivation of the venture was basically profit, not religion. It had begun in the west country of England in the early 1620s. Master White and an association of Dorchester merchants had financed a fishing settlement on Cape Ann, a rocky peninsula jutting seaward to the north and east of Boston Bay. The settlement had brought no profit, and the merchants had abandoned the enterprise. But the good master, with a few others, persevered, sending supplies to the remaining settlers—who removed from Cape Ann to what would become Salem—and searching for new financing in England. By 1628 White had interested London merchant acquaintances in the venture, and a new association had been formed. Supplies and additional men were sent to the colony that year, and in the next the association obtained a royal charter as "The Governor and Company of the Massachusetts Bay in New England." Still the intention was profit.

In the course of his agitation, however, White had spread knowledge of New England among the lay followers of Puritan preachers in England's northeastern counties. And among them, sometime in late 1628 or early 1629, talk began of utilizing the company not for profit but as a vehicle by which they could transfer themselves to New England. With whom the idea originated we cannot say. Perhaps it arose first in the household of the Earl of Lincoln at Tattershall near Sempringham; certainly that seems to have been an early center, and among the leaders of the emigration were to be Isaac Johnson, the Earl's son-in-law, Thomas Dudley, the Earl's onetime steward, and Simon Bradstreet, Dudley's son-in-law and successor as steward. But it makes little difference. By mid-1629 John Winthrop of Groton, Suffolk County, had become the one whom the "chief undertakers" would not do without, for "the

welfare of the Plantation" depended upon his going. By the
end of March, 1630, under Winthrop's leadership, the gentlemen had assumed control of the company, recruited settlers,
gathered supplies, and set sail. What is important is that the
gentlemen were children of the fellowship, sped on their
way by Master Cotton himself, who delivered the farewell
sermon, "God's Promise to His Plantation"; that the ministers
who sailed with them were from the fellowship, as were those
who would join them in New England in the years immediately after 1630; and that, given the fact that New England
during its first twenty years was "an ecclesiastical country
above any in this world"—Cotton Mather listing seventy-seven
practicing English ministers who arrived in New England in
the years to roughly 1640, John Eliot, in 1650, listing thirty-
seven practicing ministers in Massachusetts alone, one for every
415 people—New Englanders in general can be termed children
of the fellowship.[1]

The Gift in the Mind of the Recipients

Children of the fellowship? What does that mean? It is an
awkward way of saying that the New Englanders were Puritan, but the awkwardness is necessary if we are to keep in
focus the descent of their Puritanism as we have conceived it—
from the preachers *to* the laymen—and the nature of that Puritanism, that is, what they received from the ministers.

Here we are face to face with a crucial but extremely difficult problem. Our approach has been to delimit Puritanism in
terms of the preachers. We have conceptualized Puritanism as
a gift imparted to laymen who tucked it away in the storehouse of the mind, and we have described (or defined) it
while still in the possession of the giver (the preachers) in
order to avoid the confusion of trying to find the gift in the

[1] Mather, *Magnalia Christi Americana* I, 235-38; "John Eliot's Description of New England in 1650," Massachusetts Historical Society, *Pro-
ceedings*, 2d ser., II (1886), 46-50. See *infra*, n. 18.

clutter of that storehouse. But when we shift from the preacher to the layfollower, from the giver of the gift to the recipient, we move headlong toward that clutter. We ought immediately to pause and reckon up our chances of finding anything at all there. For the mind does not neatly compartmentalize things. Puritanism as we have conceived it, once conveyed to laymen, does not sit solitary on a shelf apart from all the other bric-a-brac which the mind collects and stores away. Our metaphor of gift and storehouse is convenient from the standpoint of filtering out the component influences on men, but it is erroneous when trying to envision the actual working of any single idea or set of ideas upon them. A better metaphor with which to approach the latter is the mind as a melting pot in which all the impressions and ideas collected in life (plus whatever inherited) flow together in a gooey mess—the source of that synaptic chain which leads from brain to muscle action. Psychologists, whose very subject matter is that goo, are divided over whether to plunge in or not. Insofar as he can, and admittedly he cannot for long, the poor historian had best refrain.

If we ought to forbear entering the clutter of the mind or (mixing our two metaphors) swimming in its gooey mess to analyze, what should we do? Certainly we must do more than merely describe Puritanism in terms of the preachers, for this would be to do very little. Certainly, too, we cannot simply assert that the ministers' ideas were Puritan ideas equally ascribable to ministers and laymen. This would be (and is, for historians of Puritanism frequently proceed this way) an act of faith in the efficient transmission of ideas which defies all reason—a point requiring elaboration.

It is a truism to say that what one who speaks (or writes) intends to convey is not necessarily what the man who hears (or reads) understands. Words filter through the preconceptions, values, and concerns for the particular condition of both speaker and listener. To use a simple example, a preacher might offer the phrase "saving faith" in the context of a broad theological system, using the word "saving" as a qualification —that faith which proceeds from justification and is consequently efficacious. But a listener might accept "saving" as a consequence of faith rather than a qualification—to have faith is to be saved. Or the preacher might urge godliness in the sense of the whole elaborate morphology of conversion, but the hearer might understand only the necessity for leading an outwardly moral life. The minister might condemn as sinners those who are not embarked on the Christian quest; the hearer might understand as sinners only those who frequent the public houses or the Southwark theaters and make of a negative attitude toward public houses and theaters the essence of whatever he is receiving from the preachers.[2] The idea that filters past the preconceptions, values, and particular concerns of the imparter, travels the sound waves or light rays to the recipient, filters past the recipient's own preconceptions, values, and concerns, mixes in the melting pot that constitutes the recipient's mind with all the other notions and impressions stored there, and finally moves out again to be conveyed to a third party or be transformed into action—such an idea (and all ideas follow this track) cannot retain its purity. Hence, from the layman's standpoint, the gift of Puritanism from preacher to layman can never be conceived of as anything more than an influence. We cannot, therefore, ascribe the ministers' Puritanism to the laymen and let it go at that.

And, finally, we cannot simply accept as an act of faith the assumption that the ministers' gift of Puritanism changed the lives of lay recipients so completely that what they did after

---

[2] William Prynne, for example. Note his early activity in William M. Lamont, *Marginal Prynne, 1600-1669* (London and Toronto, 1963). Interestingly enough, Thomas Lechford, in some fashion a devotee of Prynne's, was moved enough by this sort of interpretation of the preacher's gift to come to New England; but when in New England he received a deeper impression of what the preachers were saying, he turned back to English orthodoxy. See my introduction to Lechford's *Plain Dealing or News from New England* (New York and London, 1969).

receiving the gift was entirely the result of it. With regard to American Puritanism, this would lead us to the logical series:

$$\begin{array}{c}\text{Preachers'}\\ \text{Gift}\\ \text{(Puritanism)}\end{array} \rightarrow \begin{array}{c}\text{New}\\ \text{Englanders}\end{array} \rightarrow \begin{array}{c}\text{New England}\\ \text{Actions}\end{array} = \begin{array}{c}\text{Preachers'}\\ \text{Gift}\\ \text{(Puritanism)}\end{array}$$

We will not have advanced one iota from the errors suggested early in the first chapter.

MEASURING THE EFFECT OF THE GIFT

The solution to our predicament might lie in detouring around the layman's mind completely—neither enter it to attempt to analyze nor depend upon it to generalize—and concentrating on behavior. If we can establish normal patterns of life and behavior in England *without* Puritanism, deviation from the norm on the part of those *with* Puritanism might be construed as the result of that Puritan element in the lay mind which otherwise defies the historian.[3] If, for example, the normal pattern in England is to attend church four times a year, while individuals whom we can associate with Puritan preachers (hence by assumption receiving the gift of Puritanism) go four times a week, we might conceivably say that one element of the layman's Puritanism was an increased attention to churchgoing. The problems are manifold, however, and we must

---

[3] This is, of course, an expression in pure form of statistical measurement of deviation, and it is improbable that we could ever use it in such a pristine fashion. One question pinpoints the major problem: Where could we possibly find a viable base completely devoid of any possibility of Puritan influence? There is also the problem of a lack of statistical precision inherent in the nature of the materials extant from the period. We have to content ourselves with rough norms based upon England as a totality—actually, rough norms drawn from particular communities and extrapolated to English norms—counting on the size of our base to overcome the error of incorporating into the base the very deviation we want to measure. The inability to use a pristine methodology should not stop us, for one can suggest that the results will be *more* exact than results gained from extrapolation from a few items of literary evidence; it should, however, warn us against pretending that history is an exact science.

beware of them. How are we to discriminate between the effect of that with which we are concerned (Puritanism) and the effect of other but irrelevant variables? Are we to say that an effect of Puritanism is longevity if we find that the normal life-expectancy of an infant born in, say, England of 1620 is thirty-two years, while in a community served by a Puritan preacher men and women are living to an average of 71.8 years?[4] Perhaps it is true, but probably not. Common sense will be an invaluable tool. How are we to accommodate the effect of time? We saw, for example, that Puritanism in terms of the preachers was not a static but a developing thing from the 1570s to the 1630s; lay behavior emanating from Puritanism consequently cannot be static but changing. And, how are we to take into account the fact that behavior resulting from the infusion of Puritanism in the mind will vary in both degree and kind?

Let us develop this last. True, we have considered the ministerial fellowship as a rough entity, accenting common elements among preachers as a necessary step in reducing the complexity of the past generally and our concept of Puritanism specifically to manageable proportions. But here, as always, we must be aware of the intrinsic artificiality of conceptualization—the historian's ordering of the past to make it comprehensible. When we shift our attention from the common elements to the individual ministers of the fellowship, we find that each puts a peculiar stress on one or ignores another of the common elements. Thus, for one preacher a national regeneration will be paramount, and he will accent the Jeremiad, threatening and cajoling a wayward England with little reference to the dialectic of salvation. To another the dialectic will be all-important, and he will urge personal preparation and the inner search for assurance. Still a third will be

---

[4] Thirty-two is the actual life-expectancy at birth for England in the 1690s as stated by Gregory King, quoted in Peter Laslett, *The World we have lost* (New York, 1965), p. 93; Philip J. Greven, Jr., "Family Structure in Seventeenth-Century Andover, Massachusetts," *William and Mary Quarterly*, 3d ser., XXIII (1966), 239.

more concerned with the mixture of the godly and ungodly in his parish and will have traveled far along that line which led through the gathering of the godly into informal associations to the claim that such gatherings constitute the essentials of a visible church. Here a minister of the fellowship will accent the covenant which binds a gathering together and the standards which it imposes upon its members; there a minister will be more concerned with the individual faith which lies behind the gatherings. Among the ministers themselves, while in England, these differences could be balanced by the *raison d'être* of the fellowship, the necessity for those at variance with society and dissenting from the episcopacy to cling together—giving a bit more substance to the fellowship than merely a historian's artificial categorization. A man might differ but still be a friend, an ardent preacher, and a fellow worker in the Lord's vineyard, hence a companion in this ambiguous fellowship. As one minister would write of the doctrine and preaching of another, his reasons "do not satisfy me, though the man I reverence as godly and learned."[5] Among laymen associated with a Puritan preacher, however, it was the preaching not of the fellowship as a whole but of the specific preacher which had its effect, and the effect we measure by measuring the deviation of the individual or community from the norm will not be the effect of the common elements of Puritanism, but of the peculiar elements stressed by that preacher. Between "Puritan" and "Puritan," consequently, we ought to expect—and cope with—wide differences.

Moreover, we have used the phrase "associated with the preachers" perhaps too easily. Certainly it is necessary to have some clearly stipulated criteria governing who among laymen is to be considered Puritan and to keep them ever in mind, if for no other reason than to avoid the tendency to make of empirical findings based on the criteria the criteria themselves. To repeat an example already used: Laymen associated with

---

[5] Cotton to Skelton, October 2, 1630, Harris, *Memorials of . . . Dorchester*, p. 55.

Puritan preachers attend church four times a week as against the normal four times a year; increased attention to church-going is therefore an element of Puritanism. So far we are on relatively firm ground (if, of course, our empirical evidence supports us, and we rule out factors other than association with Puritan preachers as the cause of action). But to go on and say such-and-such a man (or group of men) displays an increased attendance to churchgoing and is therefore Puritan is to convert the finding into the criterion and will lead to error after error as we read additional deviation on the basis of the conversion—that is to say, from the individual or group newly defined as Puritan by the substitute criterion.[6]

But how are we to understand "associated"? Robert Keayne, to judge from his notebook, listened to Puritan preachers regularly for some seven years before leaving for New England in the early 1630s. Peter Noyes, a yeoman of the parish of Wey-hill, Hampshire, who would eventually go to Sudbury in New England, was a distant cousin of the Reverend Thomas Parker of the fellowship. Is the association of both of them with the fellowship such as to label them equally as Puritan laymen, and will their deviation from an English norm, when subjected to measurement, tell us something about Puritanism?

One caveat here is obviously to beware of a too facile association of laymen and preachers, hence too facile a choice of the individuals whose behavior and life structure are to be measured for the extent of deviation. A less obvious caveat is that degree will undoubtedly be a factor. The effect of the preachers will not be an absolute. Keayne might be deeply affected, and this be indicated in behavior, as a result of strong association; Noyes might be affected so slightly as to deviate from the normal behavior almost infinitesimally as a result of peripheral association. Moreover, degree will enter

---

[6] Some might smile at the patent ridiculousness of the error and say it cannot have occurred. But framed differently it should be familiar: Puritans are such-and-such people; such-and-such people came to New England; therefore we can read the meaning of Puritanism in New England. In the last statement we have converted the finding into the criterion.

into consideration as a result of susceptibility. Any single Englishman might cross paths with the fellowship once, twice, a hundred times or more; one contact might be enough to change his behavior, or a hundred-plus insufficient to affect him in the slightest way. And susceptibility might depend on elements otherwise irrelevant to our subject. Of three men equally associated with the fellowship, one might be so involved in satiating his desire for material wealth that he is completely unaffected; a second might be simply breaking even in this world and so look forward with a modicum of interest to the next and be affected somewhat; the third might be the proverbial loser and, giving up in this world, pin all his hopes on the next and on the good preacher who shows him the way into it.

Despite the methodological difficulties, however, we must— if we are to get anywhere at all—proceed by categorization and measurement. The caveats are simply to put us on guard, not forestop us. We can categorize New England as Puritan if such categorization implies no more than that in New England we find preachers of the fellowship and laymen in clear association with the preachers, thus maintaining the preachers and association with the preachers as our criteria of Puritanism and refraining from converting to other criteria. And we can proceed to measure the effect of Puritanism in New England *if* we accept the possibility that measurable deviation from the English norm might be accountable to irrelevant variables rather than Puritanism (geography, for example, or the exigencies of the transit of culture from old England, or simply the passage of time), and *if* we accept the further possibility of variation within New England resulting from the fact that individual ministers of the fellowship varied and that men reacted to the fellowship in different ways and to different degrees. In reading the deviation from the norm and accounting it to Puritanism it will be far safer to err by being too conservative than too liberal, that is, to account less to Puritanism than more.

A Cursory Measurement

Prima facie, we can say that some degree and kind of quickened religiosity is a part of the gift passed from preacher to laymen. One asserts this prima facie, for to do otherwise would be to argue that the preachers were singularly unsuccessful in what they considered they were about—bringing men and women to the realization of the necessity of the Christian quest as the preachers tended to define that quest. But beyond this, the data tend to conform. When we find laymen in close association with the preachers, we almost invariably find them to be more clearly religious in terms of the morphology of conversion than the average Englishman—more knowledgeable of that morphology; more diligent in pursuing religion via the preachers' principal device, the sermon; and more religiously introspective in that they were inclined to examine themselves for signs of the workings of God's will upon them.

We will return to religiosity. For the moment we need only mention it, noting further that measurement in terms of religiosity is relatively easy, particularly when religiosity is defined in terms of the specific points of polity and doctrine we have attributed to the fellowship. To go beyond religiosity, however, and call for measurement of deviation in terms of economics, or politics, or social structure is to court difficulties. The calling is easy; the accomplishment is not. In devastating fashion, historian J. H. Hexter has assaulted the "tunneling" phenomenon among historians, writing that they have "split the past into a series of tunnels, each continuous from the remote past to the present, but practically self-contained at every point and sealed off from contact with or contamination by anything that was going on in any of the other tunnels."[7] His particular bête noir was thematic tunneling—the artificial division into themes such as political history, intellectual history, economic history, social history, ad infinitum. Let us add geographic tunneling, particularly that which has divided

---

[7] J. H. Hexter, *Reappraisals in History* (Torchbook ed.; New York, 1963), p. 194.

the history of the seventeenth century as it was played out on the western shore of the Atlantic from that as played out on the eastern shore. In truth, the historian of colonial America has too often been either ignorant of all but the most general features of the work of English historians of the Tudor-Stuart-Georgian years, or he has been deluded by his search for a unique American past into believing that the crossing of the ocean or the influence of the frontier wrought such a traumatic change that one can stop at the landing beach in the quest for American beginnings. The measurement in question, however, calls for the colonial historian to break through into the Tudor-Stuart tunnel to become as familiar with the other side of the Atlantic as he is with this.

But this necessity for the colonialist to learn something new is only part of the difficulty. The simple fact is that until very recently historians—even English historians—have paid little attention to the fundamentals of sixteenth- and seventeenth-century societies. Quite rightly has Carl Bridenbaugh opened his 1968 social history of the English people for the years 1590-1642 with the line: "The ordinary men and women of any epoch of English history have seldom attracted the attention of historians." Rightly, too, has Peter Laslett, an English historian of the Tudor-Stuart years, asked:

Why is it that we know so much about the building of the British Empire, the growth of Parliament and its practices, the public and private lives of English kings, statesmen, generals, writers, thinkers and yet do not know whether all our ancestors had enough to eat? Our genealogical knowledge of how Englishmen and their distant kinsmen overseas are related to the Englishmen of the pre-industrial world is truly enormous, and is growing all the time. Why has almost nothing been done to discover how long those earlier Englishmen lived and how confident most of them could be of having any posterity at all? Not only do we not know the answers to these questions, until now we never seem to have bothered to ask them.[8]

---

[8] Carl Bridenbaugh, *Vexed and Troubled Englishmen, 1590-1642* (New York, 1968), p. vii; Laslett, *The World we have lost*, p. 127.

We can add to his questions about the society from which the New Englanders came: What sort of lives did most Englishmen of that day lead? How did society operate on a day-to-day basis? What were the assumptions of the men in England's village lanes and town streets? Without the answers we have no English norm from which to measure, and we are only now beginning to find the answers.

We do, however, have data for the New England side of the Atlantic, although not nearly enough along certain lines. Lengthy tomes have elaborately dissected the "mind" of New England, and if the dissection has been based only on the writings of a few leading laymen and clerics, it nevertheless clearly delineates the publicly pronounced values and assumptions of those few.[9] We have, too, voluminous works elaborately portraying various aspects of New England society—the family; the workings of towns, villages, and churches; the law; manners and morals; servants and town officers; crime and punishment. Yet the one blind generalization that New England is Puritan and that therefore all that we find in New England is Puritan clouds the view. If we glimpse a criminal being turned off the ladder in Boston in the 1630s or 1640s, we do not put it down as simply English justice being done but *Puritan* justice; if a law is discerned which limits wages or prices, it is immediately labeled a *Puritan* law; and if we discern a strong family orientation with domination by the father, we refer to familialism and the patriarch as elements of *Puritanism.*

With the basic facts of English life only now being studied in depth and of New England life too rashly generalized as Puritan, any attempt at measurement is begun impropitiously. But we can begin, using what we are slowly understanding about the former (English life) and what we know of the latter (New England). And to proceed is to be immediately struck by a curious impression: With the exception of religious

---

[9] Rutman, "Mirror of Puritan Authority," in Billias, ed., *Law and Authority,* p. 163.

attitudes and institutions (which we will take up later) the measurable difference between New and old England which need be accounted for by the influence of the preaching fellowship—our criterion for Puritanism—is minimal! Simply put, nothing in the way of social or political policy discernible in New England is not to be found pervasive in old England. It cannot be stressed in strong enough language that this conclusion is tentative and that it is based upon only the beginnings of deep research into the ordinary lives of Englishmen. But with one after another of the "Puritan" traits being revealed as nothing more than English traits, one can hardly avoid suggesting that further work in English social history will merely add to the impression.

Let us exemplify the case in the simplest way possible. What follows is a sampling of statements from historians of New England society; appended to the right are statements about Tudor-Stuart English society in general, all drawn from a single work by social historian Peter Laslett:

New England[10]	*England*[11]
[Note] the often repeated Puritan warning that every man, for the good of society, must remain	In this society, subordination and politics were founded on tradition. . . . This submissive

[10] Edmund S. Morgan, ed., *Puritan Political Ideas, 1558-1794* (Indianapolis, 1965), p. xvii; Bushman, *Puritan to Yankee*, p. 14; Morgan, *Puritan Family*, pp. 76-77; Thomas Jefferson Wertenbaker, *The Puritan Oligarchy: The Founding of American Civilization* (New York and London, 1947), pp. 42-44; Ola Elizabeth Winslow, *Meetinghouse Hill, 1630-1783* (New York, 1952), pp. 50-51; Stuart Bruchey, ed., *The Colonial Merchant* (New York, 1966), pp. 91-92; Joseph Gaer and Ben Siegel, *The Puritan Heritage* (New York, 1964), p. 87; Edmund S. Morgan, "The Puritans and Sex," in Carl N. Degler, ed., *Pivotal Interpretations of American History* (New York, 1966), I, 6. In all fairness it must be added that in some cases the authors of these passages go on to note the English custom, Morgan writing for example that "the custom of placing children in other families already existed in England in the sixteenth century." But the context of the discussions, the constant reiteration of the adjective "Puritan," and the casualness of the admission of the English custom (when admitted), all tend to sublimate the parallel custom to the notion of a peculiar Puritan attribute.

[11] Laslett, *The World we have lost*, pp. 173-74, 177-78, 19-20, 12, 60, 74, 118, 35, 130.

New England (Cont.)

in the place to which God had called him. [Governor] Winthrop could remind the emigrants to Massachusetts that God had so ordered the condition of mankind that 'in all times some must be rich some poore, some highe and eminent in power and dignitie; others meane and in subjection,' and he was properly shocked when a servant suggested to a master who was unable to pay him that they change places.

Weakness in the family endangered the entire social order, for the Puritans knew that the pattern of submission set in the home fixed the attitude toward authority throughout life and that strong family government prevented disorder in the state. The father was the model for all authority—magistrates were called the fathers of their people —and the biblical commandment to honor parents was expanded to include all rulers.

England (Cont.)

cast of mind is almost universal in the statements made by the men about themselves. 'There is degree above degree, As reason is . . .' 'Take but degree away, Untune that string, And hark what discord follows.' It would seem that once a man in the traditional world got himself into a position where he could catch a glimpse of his society as a whole, he immediately felt that degree, order, was its essential feature. Without degree, unquestioning subordination, and some men being privileged while all the others obeyed, anarchy and destruction were inevitable. Any threat to the established order was a danger to everyone's personality.

The duty of Christian obedience rested on the commandment *Honour thy Father and thy Mother.* . . . What more familiar sentiment for the beneficed rector or the itinerant preacher to appeal to when the children of the village community were being instructed in their Christian duties? Submission to the powers that be went very well with the habit of obedience to the head of the patriarchal family, and it had the extremely effective sanction of the universal fear of damnation to the defiant. 'Short life,' so the doctrine went, 'was the punishment of disobedient children.'

New England (Cont.)

To strengthen control at the primary level, the General Assembly ordered that every young person submit himself to family government.

Puritan children were frequently brought up in other families than their own even when there was no apparent educational [or economic] advantage involved. . . . In explanation I suggest that Puritan parents did not trust themselves with their own children, that they were afraid of spoiling them by too great affection.

It could not have been by chance that each group of settlers turned to the English manor as the model for their town, not in political or religious matters, but in its agricultural, industrial and, to some extent, social features. The manor was a dying institution in England. . . . Their natural impulse would have been to ignore this relic of medieval times, and divide their land into farms. But against this, it seems certain, their advisors warned them in the

England (Cont.)

Only the recognition that people came not as individuals, but as families, makes it possible to begin to come closer to the facts. . . . It goes without saying, of course, that no one in a position of 'service' was an independent member of society, national or local. . . . Such men and women, boys and girls, were caught up, so to speak, 'subsumed' is the ugly word we shall use, into the personalities of their fathers and masters.

Sometimes, we have found, [the ordinary Englishman] would prefer to send out his own children as servants and bring in other children and young men to do the work. This is one of the few glimpses we can get into the quality of the emotional life of the family at this time, for it shows that parents may have been unwilling to submit children of their own to the discipline of work at home.

Though the detailed arrangements for the working of the land were no longer undertaken at the manor court, and though that court might be dying as an institution, nevertheless, the community still had its affairs to run co-operatively. The church had to be administered. . . . The poor law had to be carried out; the roads had to be kept up; the constable appointed to maintain the peace. The more important the common responsibilities of

New England (Cont.)

most emphatic terms, pointing out that to scatter themselves throughout their town would not only militate against the unity so essential to a new community, but might so discourage the advancement of religion as to defeat the chief purpose of their migration.... The creation of the agricultural village is a tribute to the foresight of Winthrop, or Dudley, or Endicott, or whoever it was that thought this matter through, for it became the corner stone of Puritan New England.

On Sunday it was always 'going to meeting' or 'going to preaching'; never going to church. In the town mind, as well as on the Town Book, this was not God's holy temple; it was an all-purpose place of assembly. In a typical phrase which expressed the current view for more than a century it was 'our meeting-house, built by our own vote, framed by our own hammers and saws, and by our own hands set in the convenientest place for us all.' Accordingly, no particular sacredness attached to the building itself. On Sunday the town assembled here for preach-

England (Cont.)

any community, presumably, the stronger the association between its members, because each one's interest is engaged. But living together in one township, isolated, spatially, from others of comparable size, of very much the same structure, inevitably means a communal sense and communal activity. . . . The strength of this sense of community in the English villager can be seen when he removed himself beyond the ocean, and settled again, surrounded by the alien, virgin land, which required new household groupings. In the final years of the traditional order in England, when the English were establishing their townships on the eastern seaboard of the North American continent, the village community at home was of course the model.

Every meeting of the village community took place in the Church.... This function of the church building as a meeting place for all the purposes of the community, must be stressed. Here they were, these farming householders, not all of whom could read, sitting in the building put up by their fore-runners many centuries before, and which they, in their turn, annually repaired and even beautified. In the place where they came so often to Christian service they chose their neighbors for the traditional offices, secular and spiritual. When English

New England (Cont.)

ing; on town meeting Monday essentially, the same group met in the same place to vote 'fence repairs,' convenient 'Horse Bridges,' rings for swine. . . .

Agrarian in outlook and deeply religious, they strongly supported the emphasis of the church on the restrictive elements within the Puritan heritage [with regard to economics]. . . . Note particularly the provision for selectmen 'to set reasonable rates upon all commodities and proportionately to limit the wages of workmen and labourers.'

Even the well-covered woman was not beyond censure or punishment if her attire was considered too expensive, affected, or simply beyond her social station. Such indulgence was a clear indication of overweening pride. This applied also to men.

Toward sexual intercourse outside marriage the Puritans were as frankly hostile as they were favorable to it in marriage. They passed laws to punish adultery with death, and fornication with whippings. Yet they had no misconceptions as to the capacity of human beings to obey such laws.

England (Cont.)

villagers found themselves in America, one of the first buildings which they put up for the new village was the *Meeting House,* for the town meeting had a great deal to decide in starting all anew. The *Meeting House* was also, of course, the Christian church of the village being born.

Once we are alive to the real possibility of famine the perpetual preoccupation of the authorities of that era, governmental and municipal, with the supply of food for the poor takes on a new significance. The insistence on fair prices for all victuals and especially of bread is a reminder that people might starve even where supplies were available. . . . Hence the strict control of all dealings in breadstuffs and all handlers of them.

Private correspondence is full of resentment at common people wearing the clothes reserved to the socially superior.

The code of moral behaviour in the traditional world can be looked upon . . . as an essential part of the workings of the general social scheme. Here was a nation-wide community of persons . . . living under agrarian conditions and not far above subsistence level. It was a com-

New England (Cont.)

Although the laws were commands of God, it was only natural—since the fall of Adam—for human beings to break them. Breaches must be punished lest the community suffer the wrath of God.

England (Cont.)

munity which made of the nuclear family the unit for nearly all activity, only adding other persons to it as servants, when that was necessary. If the shape of the society was to be maintained, Pauline morality had to be enforced.... Ordinary people can rarely be heard on this subject. But when they spoke their minds as witnesses in ecclesiastical courts they left no doubt that sexual intercourse outside marriage was universally condemned.

Enough of juxtaposing of quotations. To continue would undoubtedly bore the reader without materially adding to the clear impression that New England, considered apart from religion, far from being a distinct culture, its deviation from the English norm subject to ready measurement, was really—to use Laslett's word—traditional within that English norm.

NEW ENGLAND AND VIRGINIA: TRADITION AND INNOVATION

Let us see the situation clearly and, for a moment, widen our sights to include areas other than New England to which Englishmen went in the seventeenth century. Englishmen settling in New England seem to have tended to reestablish as closely as possible the traditional culture which, through the works of such as Laslett, we are now beginning to understand. Did all Englishmen do this? Apparently not. The Virginians do not seem to have. They did not settle in communities, did not—and I paraphrase Laslett here only to indicate that the restrictions of tunnel history work both ways, that he seems to know as little about the western shore of the Atlantic as colonial historians know of the eastern—did not establish townships using the village community of England as the model, did not construct as one of their first buildings a meetinghouse and troop in periodically to deal with the multifarious business incumbent in starting anew. Indeed, we can interpret various actions (all abortive) of the Virginia Company of London and later of the crown as attempts to induce artificially the traditional culture—the imposition, for example, of semimartial (can we call it patriarchal?) law in the early years of the colony, the periodic attempts to have Virginians abandon their dispersed population pattern and congregate in towns. Of course, this is only a surface glance. Historians have not yet penetrated very far into any seventeenth-century Anglo-American society except that of New England. There might well be—to use but one example—traditional family attitudes and patterns hidden in the extant records. But this surface glance would certainly seem to indicate that the Virginians were *a*-traditional, that their culture was something new in the English-speaking world and in sharp contrast to the traditional New England culture—this despite the more general view which considers the Virginians the transplanters par excellence.[12] One can, in effect, suggest a reversal of the normal way of dealing with New England and Virginia. New England differed from Virginia not because the Virginians were typically English and the New Englanders were trying to make a new (and to their lights a better) society, but because the New Englanders were transplanting a traditional society and the Virginians were straying from the traditional.

If one accepts this reversal, one immediately comes to the question of causation. Why did the Virginians stray from the tradition? Why did the New Englanders remain within the tradition? The answer is certainly not simplistic. It involves, of course, the concept of cultural baggage: Men brought their social· and cultural experiences with them to the New World and, in building anew, built with what they knew; they would deviate from the known only under pressure; cultural inertia, consequently, was a force for the traditional.[13] But the an-

12 Daniel Boorstin, *The Americans: The Colonial Experience* (New York, 1958), Pt. 4.
13 Robert F. Berkhofer, Jr., "Space, Time, Culture and the New Frontier," *Agricultural History*, XXVIII (1964), 24-25.

swer might also involve the very nature of initial settlement—
by individuals in Virginia (recall that the very first settlers
were all males), by families (in terms certainly of influence if
not numbers) in New England. And the answer might well
involve geography or agricultural systems. New England's
agriculture, as it developed, was little different from old England's agriculture; indeed, what drove New England into com-
mercial endeavors seems to have been the fact that the section
produced exactly the same commodities that old England produced, and that as a consequence the section had to take to
the sea to find non-English markets for its produce.[14] Virginia's
agriculture came to center on a system of tobacco cultivation
alien to England. A traditional society could fit New England's traditional agriculture; a new society had to evolve to
encompass the new agriculture of Virginia. We cannot, however, discount the possibility that the answer might involve
Puritanism as well—the Christian fellowship.

Earlier in this chapter—specifically at the close of the first
section—we noted that the gentlemen who led the Winthrop
migration were children of the fellowship, that the ministers
who sailed with them and in the years immediately following
were from the fellowship, and that by 1650 the number of
practicing ministers in Massachusetts alone was thirty-seven,
one for every 415 people. What of Virginia? True, the fellowship touched that colony in its earliest years. Ships arriving in England in November 1609, reported that "unhappy
dissension" had fallen out among the settlers "by reason of
their Minister, who being, as they say, somewhat a Puritan,
the most part refused to go to his services and hear his sermons, though by the other part he was supported and fa-

---

[14] Darrett B. Rutman, "Governor Winthrop's Garden Crop: The Significance of Agriculture in the Early Commerce of Massachusetts Bay,"
William and Mary Quarterly, 3d ser., XX (1963), 396-415.

vored."[15] Master Alexander Whitaker arrived on the James River in 1611 and died in 1617. Family and education link Whitaker to the fellowship. (Among his uncles was Laurence Chaderton.) And from Virginia, Whitaker wrote to others of the fellowship, his letters marked by the very spirit of the group. There were, too, other ministers in early Virginia who can be linked, although only tentatively in some cases, to the fellowship.[16] Yet this entry into the South never developed. In the face of Virginia's succession of disasters none of the earliest ministers was blessed with longevity. There were always too few ministers for the size and dispersal of the colony's population. And, as in England, as Anglicanism rose vis-à-vis dissent, the government in Virginia tended to brand the few ministers of the fellowship who arrived as dissenters and exercise the law against them. One effect of this was to leave even fewer ministers in Virginia than there might otherwise have been. In 1649 a group of newcomers, arriving after a particularly hazardous journey from England at the home of a settler in Northampton County on Virginia's Eastern Shore, thought to give thanks in a church for a safe arrival. It was Sunday and "we would have been glad to have found a church for the performance of our duty to God," one wrote; "to have rendered our hearty thanks to him in the public assembly . . .; but we were not yet arrived in the heart of the country where there were churches, and ministry performed."[17] The writer erred only in thinking that things would be better

---

[15] J. Beaulieu to William Trumbull, November 30, 1609, Trumbull MSS, Berkshire Record Office, utilizing microfilm in the Virginia Colonial Records Project, Virginia State Library, Richmond.

[16] Harry Culverwell Porter, "Alexander Whitaker: Cambridge Apostle to Virginia," *William and Mary Quarterly*, 3d ser., XIV (1957), 317-43; Alexander Brown, ed., *The Genesis of the United States* (London, 1890), I, 497 ff.; George Maclaren Brydon, *Virginia's Mother Church and the Political Conditions under Which It Grew* (Richmond and Philadelphia, 1947-52), I, chap. 4; Miller, *Errand into the Wilderness*, chap. 4.

[17] Colonel Norwood, *A Voyage to Virginia*, in Peter Force, comp., *Tracts and Other Papers Relating Principally to the Origin, Settlement, and Progress of the Colonies in North America* (Peter Smith ed.; Gloucester, Mass., 1963), III, Tract 10, p. 48.

"in the heart of the country." For in all Virginia at that moment there were only six ministers, one per 3,239 persons.[18]

Clearly the presence of ministers in large numbers relative to the population in New England and the absence of ministers in any significant numbers in Virginia is a measurable distinction between the two areas. If we assume that ministers generally are a force for traditional social organization and behavior, for traditional culture, the distinction can be worked into the explanation for the fact that New England found its way into traditional organization and behavior while Virginia deviated. The ministers' voice was, in New England, added to the force of cultural inertia, initial settlement by families, and the agricultural potential; the lack of a ministerial voice in Virginia in effect removed an impediment to straying from the traditional when other factors (initial settlement by individuals and tobacco-based agriculture) encouraged that straying. But we might go one step farther. Perhaps the voice of the fellowship—as the laymen heard it—was more loudly a voice for tradition than that of the ordinary minister. If this was the case, we should expect that New England would be more intensely traditional than even England, our norm. And perhaps the very intensity of adherence to tradition is a deviation from that norm which we ought to seize upon as a primary effect of the preachers' gift upon the lay mind.

---

[18] Based upon a survey of known ministers in the colony, the principal sources for which are Edmond Neill, *Notes on the Virginia Clergy* (Philadelphia, 1877); Edward L. Goodwin, *The Colonial Church in Virginia* (Milwaukee, 1927); George M. Brydon, "Addendum to Goodwin's List of Colonial Clergy . . .," typescript, Virginia State Library, Richmond; Frederick L. Weis, *The Colonial Clergy of Virginia, North Carolina, and South Carolina* (Boston, 1955); and the author's own research. Population figures for both Virginia and New England are, of course, best estimates and subject to the many reservations stipulated in the author's *Winthrop's Boston: Portrait of a Puritan Town, 1630-1649* (Chapel Hill, N. C. 1965), pp. 293-94.

CHAPTER 3

CHILDREN OF TRADITION

In our first chapter we set the bounds of Puritanism in terms of the Christian fellowship of preachers as it emerged in late sixteenth- and early seventeenth-century England. In our second we considered some of the difficulties of approaching lay as against clerical Puritanism. But we were able to suggest at least two possible aspects of the preachers' gift to laymen associated with them—some degree and kind of quickened religiosity and an exaggerated concern for social values discerned as traditional. We shall turn to religiosity in our next chapter; here let us explore this suggestion of exaggerated traditionalism.

The English Idealization of Society

We must begin by separating out several threads from the fabric of early seventeenth-century England—the first, the prevalent idealization of society.

Order—the hierarchical arrangement of society by which men stood in seried ranks, in proper and natural relationships of higher and lower, authority and subordination—was venerated. Authority pronounced it, educated Englishmen reading in their Aristotle: "Authority and subordination are conditions not only inevitable but also expedient . . . because in every composite thing where a plurality of parts, whether continuous or discrete, is combined to make a single whole," such as a community or society, "there is always found a ruling and a subject factor."[1] So too with religion. Thus from the homilies appointed to be read in every church in England:

> Almighty God hath created and appointed all things, in heaven, earth, and waters, in a most excellent and perfect order. In heaven he hath appointed distinct (or several) orders, and states of archangels and angels. In earth, he hath assigned and appointed kings and princes, with other governors under them, all in good and necessary order. The water above is kept, and raineth down in due time and season. The sun, moon, stars, rainbow, thunder, lightning, clouds, and all birds of the air, do keep their order. The earth, trees, seeds, plants, herbs, corn, grass and all manner of beasts, keep themselves in their order. . . . And man himself also hath all his parts both within and without, as soul, heart, mind, memory, understanding, reason, speech, with all and singular corporal members of his body, in a profitable, necessary and pleasant order. Every degree of people, in their vocations, calling, and office, hath appointed to them their duty and order. Some are in high degree, some in low; some kings and princes, some inferiors and subjects; priests and laymen, masters and servants, fathers and children, husbands and wives, rich and poor; and every one have need of other.[2]

Translated into action via the catechism of 1549—still read in most churches in the 1630s—this meant very simply, "my duty . . . [is] to submit myself to all my governors, teachers, spiritual pastors and masters; to order myself lowly and reverently to all my betters, : . . not to covet nor desire other men's goods: but to learn and labor truly to get my own living, and

---

[1] Quoted in Anthony Esler, *The Aspiring Mind of the Elizabethan Younger Generation* (Durham, N.C., 1966), p. 34.

[2] "An Exhortation to Obedience," *The Book of Homilies* (1562), in Society for the Propagation of the Christian Church, *Certain Sermons or Homilies* (London, 1890), p. 109.

do my duty in that state of life unto which it shall please God
to call me."[3] Shakespeare echoed this sense of order:

> The heavens themselves, the planets and this centre,
> Observe degree, priority and place.
> ... O, when degree is shaked,
> Which is the ladder of all high designs,
> The enterprise is sick! How could communities ...
> Prerogative of age, crowns, sceptres, laurels,
> But by degree, stand in authentic place?

And another playwright, Robert Greene, called down punishment on those who, led by ambition, would violate it:

> Exile, torment, and punish such as they;
> For greater vipers never may be found
> Within a state than such aspiring heads,
> That reck not how they climb, so that they climb.[4]

Men ideally stood not only in ordered ranks, but by families
broadly defined. In a sense society was envisioned in terms of
children and adults, although these concepts had a different interpretation than we would give them. Adults were men (of
varying degrees in terms of the social hierarchy) with wives
and land—a cottage little better than a cattleshed with a modicum of land about or a manor house with broad acres, it
mattered not. Children were all the rest above infancy, what
we would call "children" plus adolescents and young men and
women, even young adults. The line of separation was not
age but the house and land, the holding of which allowed one a
wife and progeny; childhood was not biological but economic
and social. The French scholar Philippe Ariès, whose work has
done more than anything else to open our minds to the early
modern family, put it very aptly in his *Centuries of Childhood*:
"The idea of childhood was bound up with the idea of dependence. . . . One could leave childhood only by leaving the state

---

[3] Quoted in Laslett, *The World we have lost*, p. 176.

[4] *Troilus and Cressida*, act I, scene iii, lines 86-87, 101-3, 107-8; Greene,
The Scottish History of James the Fourth, act II, lines 2413-16, in J. C.
Collins, ed., *Plays and Poems of Robert Greene* (Oxford, 1905).

of dependence."[5] We can reverse his thought: Adulthood was tied to the idea of independence. And we can carry it a step further: Those who counted in the society were independent family men; the children—the dependents—crowded in where they could. Some worked with fathers until fathers should pass away and the holding pass to the son who then assumed wife, independent standing, and adulthood. Others worked in the houses of those of higher degree, or as apprentices and journeymen in trades, familial dependents in this context. Moreover, if dependency was a subjugation of self to a "father," real or symbolic (such as the apprentice's master), "father-hood" entailed an obligation to preserve, protect, and nurture the "child." The obligation was mournfully put by Cervantes —and notably we are dealing with a European and not strictly English idea—when he described Don Quixote's thoughts as the old warrior for traditional values gazed on the sleeping Sancho:

> Sleep, you have no worries. You have committed the respon-sibility for your person to my shoulders; it is a burden which nature and tradition have imposed on those who have ser-vants. The valet sleeps while the master sits up, wondering how to *feed him, improve him, and do good to him.*[6]

Society—that of the village or town, or of England as a whole —was envisioned as an interdependent web, a unified network of families committed, for whatever the ultimate end, to main-taining the well-being of the total society, indeed, even to the degree of sublimating the individual to the good of the whole. The rhetoric of order and degree, of every man in his place in one social body, led inexorably to the image of men, from their individual places within families, sacrificing their own in-terests to the whole. Thus a common analogy was that between society and the human body in which the lowly foot was con-tent to perform the duties of a foot and not covet the position of the lofty head. The analogy was readily extended: The

---

[5] *Centuries of Childhood: A Social History of Family Life,* Robert Baldick, trans. (New York, 1962), p. 26.

[6] Quoted in *ibid.,* p. 397.

foot sacrifices itself against sharp rocks if running over
rocks is the only way to escape a wild beast and so save
whole body. It was within this context that Edward Fo
landowner and justice of the peace, wrote: "The wealth,
power and goodness whatsoever of every particular p
must be conferred and reduced to the common good."[7] But even
beyond the exaltation of community and sublimation of self
lay an assumption that in the interconnection of families was
the very cement of the community. "As Adam was lord of
his children," Sir Robert Filmer wrote in his *Patriarcha*, "so his
children under him had a command over their own children.
. . . I see not then how the children of Adam, or of any man
else, can be free from subjection to their parents. And this
subordination of children is the fountain of all . . . authority."[8]

Order and a family structure of society, diligence in one's
place and a subsuming of self to the good of the whole, and,
inherent in all that has been said, the notion of the oneness of
the social body, of the organic unity of society which, while
accepting functional differences between parts, always considered the sum of the parts paramount—these, far too briefly
put, were the key elements of the Elizabethan/Jacobean idealization of society, bequeathed to that age by an earlier time and
hence referred to here as traditional. Like all ideals, these
emanated from an attempt to rationalize a reality, in this case
originally a medieval reality, perceived, rationalized, and cast
into an evaluative framework largely by the medieval church.[9]
The rationalization never quite fit that earlier reality, however,
and, society being ever-changing, the gap between the rationalization and reality became larger and larger as time pro⌐

---

[7] *A Comparative Discourse . . . Wherein Out of the Principles of Nature Is Set Forth the True Frame of a Commonwealth* (1606), quoted in
J. W. Allen, *English Political Thought, 1603-1644* (London, 1938), p. 81.

[8] *Patriarcha and Other Political Works of Sir Robert Filmer*, Peter
Laslett, ed. (Oxford, 1949), p. 57. See also Laslett's introduction, but
note that in his subsequent work he corrects the erroneous view of an
actual "extended" family system which he here assumes.

[9] R. H. Tawney, *Religion and the Rise of Capitalism* (London, 1926),
chap. I.

gressed. Nevertheless men—Englishmen as the seventeenth century opened—still perceived and evaluated their society in such terms, casting the reality they discerned against the traditional ideal.

CHANGE—REAL AND PERCEIVED—AND A DISCOMFITED AGE

Out of a contrast of ideal and perceived reality in early seventeenth-century England we pluck a second necessary thread—a sense of discomfiture, of vexation (as historian Carl Bridenbaugh has called it),[10] a vague feeling in some, a rather precise feeling in others, that all was not well with England.

More often than not American students, contemplating that England from which America had its first beginnings, think in terms of the swashbuckling Drake, the mercantile dreams of the two Richard Hakluyts, and the nationalism of Shakespeare. But these represent only a part of the scene. England of the moment was changing. We must not overstate the case and say that England, from being medieval, was becoming modern. Nor must we understate the case and simply consider England as a static society awaiting industrialization in order to become modern. Both have been done. We must simply acknowledge that there was change, some real and some in the minds of men, and that change was disconcerting.

The kingdom was changing religiously, as we have seen, and in that change the clerics of the kingdom were dividing into a Puritan and non-Puritan ministry. The political institutions were changing, and Parliament and Court were increasingly in open confrontation. There was economic change. England's population was spurting upwards; towns and cities—London particularly—were growing; prices were rising and markets were shifting; land was available for purchase and lease at a rate unheard of a century earlier. And economic changes were producing contrasts and departures from old ways in the society at large.

---

[10] In his *Vexed and Troubled Englishmen*, cited *supra*.

The economy, while expanding, was as yet unable to accommodate comfortably the increased number of people. Hence, while vibrant and rich in opportunity—as befitted an expanding economy—England was plagued by the poor and dispossessed. And while the kingdom found ways to accommodate those who rose to opportunity and succeeded, it had not yet—nor would it for long—develop a social conscience which could accommodate failures. Thus the countryside was being literally rebuilt as prospering yeomen and gentry remodeled or replaced the medieval cottages and great halls of their fathers —this on the one hand. On the other, a survey of the single town of Sheffield in 1625 labeled 725 of the 2,207 inhabitants "begging poor."[11] A knighthood might be purchased by a well-to-do yeoman, a peerage by a successful merchant's son (and notably in this inflation of honors, honors were being demeaned in a society which tended to venerate honors).[12] But a sheriff's or constable's whip more often than not honored the back of the poor who left their villages by the thousands to wander.

Success and failure—this was but one of the many contrasts in England. In the countryside was an inherent and longstanding contrast between village structures. In some areas one found a rurality dominated by hamlets and single farmsteads with little sense of community and but a minimum of community discipline, where men tended to live dispersed, apart from one another, enclosing their land in individual farms and working it as they would. In other areas the countryside was dominated by nucleated, highly organized villages surrounded by open fields worked more or less as a common endeavor by villagers living compactly and with greater orientation toward community and less toward the individual—the "tightly knit, strong-spirited community of tenants, farmers,

---

[11] W. G. Hoskins, "The Rebuilding of Rural England, 1570-1640," *Past & Present*, IV (1953), 44-57; John D. Leader, ed., *Records of the Burgery of Sheffield* (London, 1897), pp. 135-36.

[12] Lawrence Stone, *The Crisis of the Aristocracy, 1558-1641* (Oxford, 1965), chap. III.

and parishioners" which historian Sumner Chilton Powell ascribed to one emigrant to New England.[13] Such contrasts were compounded now as villages of both types changed in response to the changing economy. And contrasts, old and new, were exaggerated as personal horizons expanded with the movement of men from one village to another and to towns and cities in pursuit of the main chance. (One historian has estimated that in 1641 only 16 per cent of the agricultural population had been a hundred years in the same locality.)[14] For us today expanding horizons would seem an advance over a time when most men knew only their immediate community, a healthy sign of progress. But consider the man removed from what was to him traditional life and shown equally traditional or changing lives being lived in areas, perhaps just over the next hill, once isolated from him. The expanding horizons present contrasts between a known and unknown, variety where once there existed in the mind but one traditional order.

In the towns and cities there were contrasts too. Again there were those between the successful and the failures. There were contrasts between old and new citizens, between old and new enterprises. And perhaps most important there was contrast between an older and a newer way of business. The former was that of the artisan or shopkeeper whose place of work was his home, whose journeymen, apprentices, and maidservants were as much "family" as were wife and children, and who lived complacently and comfortably within a scheme which considered his work as much a social service as a way for private gain.[15] The latter—the contrast—was to be found in what one writer has called "the new technique of money-making," another has labelled "economic individualism," a third

---

[13] H. P. R. Finberg, ed., *The Agrarian History of England and Wales,* IV, *1500-1640,* Joan Thirsk, ed. (Oxford, 1967), chap. I; Sumner Chilton Powell, *Puritan Village: The Formation of a New England Town* (Middletown, Conn., 1963), p. 11.

[14] E. E. Rich, "The Population of Elizabethan England," *Economic History Review,* 2d ser., II (1950), 261.

[15] Well described in the opening paragraphs of Laslett, *The World we have lost.*

has equated with the rise of London-centered monopolists and investment merchants, and some men of the time discerned and feared as a too successful voraciousness, a sense of self in business which denied the claims of family, society, charity, even conscience, and yet seemed to reward its practitioners with success. "Who is he that will not make of his own the best he can?" a fictional merchant of the new persuasion asked in a pamphlet of the day. "A covetous man," Sir Thomas Overbury answered, one whose "actions are guilty of more crimes than any other men's thoughts," who "conceives no sin which he dare not act save only lust, from which he abstains for fear he should be charged with keeping bastards," whose usury "is doubled, and no sixpence begot or born but presently, by an untimely thrift, it is getting more," "who never spends candle but at Christmas . . . in hope that his servants will break glasses for want of light, which they double pay for in their wages."[16]

In but a few paragraphs one can hardly do justice to the change and sense of change, the apparent contrasts and departures from old ways, which marked England. One must note this aspect of England, however, in order to hold it against the prevalent idealization of society. Where was the proper unity and ordering of society when lowly priests bickered with bishops, when Parliament and King argued—a double break in the social ideal, for if the men of Parliament controverted the King and hence the sense of order, their contravention was obliged by a king who was not playing the proper father to the family which the kingdom was envisioned to be? Where order when upstart courtiers and merchants lorded their new rank or new wealth among their betters, or when country bumpkins come into a little money aped the manners of the gentry even to the purchase of a knighthood?

[16] S. T. Bindoff, *Tudor England* (Harmondsworth, Eng., 1950), p. 131; Christopher Hill, *The Century of Revolution, 1603-1714* (New York, 1961), pp. 20 ff.; Tawney, *Religion and the Rise of Capitalism*, pp. 178-79; Sir Thomas Overbury, *Many Witty Characters and Conceited News* (1614) in Isobel Bowman, ed., *A Theatre of Natures: Some XVII Century Character Writings* (London, 1955), pp. 80-81.

Where was the thought of sublimating oneself to the good of the whole when, at least to some, so many men sought their own gain, when ambition, greed, and avarice were such common sins as to be no sins at all, or when other men (the beggars) contributed nothing to society and devoted themselves to the sins of laziness and sloth? Where was the sense of family when theoretically-dependent children assumed untoward independence as they left the villages of their birth to find land elsewhere or entered the towns and cities to find trades; where the obligation toward servants when servants were considered mere menials to be exploited? In such questions, in the contrast of a discerned reality and an idealization of society, men found discomfort in England. And as more men were educated to the rhetoric of the ideal—for notably education was on the rise in this England and the "textbooks" of the time gave formal expression to the ideal—more men were asking the questions and feeling the discomfort.[17] Far from a panacea, education was an exacerbation. Men who would live according to the ideal found it increasingly difficult; those who would live contrary found the ideal in their way; and any who would cast their own times against the ideal found their times tarnished in the comparison.

This sense of a tarnished age is to be found in literature. Thus Anthony Esler, writing of the "melancholy malcontents" of the late Elizabethan, early Jacobean years, quotes Shakespeare's Hamlet:

. . . this goodly frame, the earth, seems to me a
sterile promontory;

and John Marston's Bruto:

. . . Oh thou corrupted age,
Which slight regard'st men of sound carriage;
Virtue, knowledge, fly to heaven again
Deign not among those ungrateful sots remain.[18]

---

[17] Lawrence Stone, "The Educational Revolution in England, 1560-1640," *Past & Present*, XXVIII (1964), 41-80.

[18] Esler, *The Aspiring Mind of the Elizabethan Younger Generation*, pp. 238, 240.

Bridenbaugh quotes Thomas Dekker:

> To cosen[19] and be cosen'd makes the age.
> The prey and feeder are that civil thing
> That sager heads call body politic.[20]

It is to be found in the writings of popular pamphleteers such as Thomas Nashe, who both mercilessly mocked the aspiring climber and just as mercilessly condemned the wandering beggar, and catalogued a compendium of social sins from ambition and greed, lust and avarice, to sloth and laziness.[21] And it is to be found in the writings of the preachers of our Christian fellowship. They, too, were discomfited by their age.

THE JEREMIAD OF THE FELLOWSHIP

We have already, in our first chapter, noted the phenomenon: the preachers of the fellowship increasingly at variance with society about them in terms of religion, particularly at variance with the hierarchy of the church, not abandoning England but bitterly critical, their sermons echoes of the biblical Jeremiah. For the most part the preachers' criticism emanated from what they conceived to be irreligion—Sabbath-breaking, for example—and from their estrangement from the established authorities of the church. The fact that this estrangement was increasing in the seventeenth century and most notably in the 1620s resulted in a quickened tempo to the Jeremiad. The faint beginnings of Anglicanism discernible in the theological disputes at Cambridge in the 1590s were culminating in the Anglicanism of William Laud, appointed bishop of St. David's in 1621, translated to Bath and Wells in 1626, to London in 1628, and ultimately named archbishop of Canterbury in 1633. As the Anglicanism personified by Laud captured the hierarchy and so made official its tempered Calvinism, the preachers

---

[19] I.e., "cheat."
[20] Bridenbaugh, *Vexed and Troubled Englishmen*, p. 362.
[21] See Nashe's *Pierce Penilesse his Supplication to the Divell* (London, 1592).

became more vocally Calvinistic. As Anglicanism accented ceremonialism and formalism, some preachers shrieked of a turning back toward Roman Catholicism and held out the fate of Protestant churches in Bohemia and France falling to a Catholic resurgence by way of grim prophecy. And as Anglicanism asserted the divine nature of the episcopacy which it was capturing and from its seat of power demanded conformity to its ways on the part of the preachers, threatening deprivation or silencing for nonconformity, one after another of the preachers sharpened their arguments against episcopacy. "What hath God found in England?" a preacher of 1628 asked. "Formality, Drunkenness, falling from God to popery, idolatry."

> He looks for obedience but beholds rebellion, contempt. He looks that we should be brought to a right frame by all our [past] blessings, his pains, his judgments [in our behalf]. He looks we should wait on God and come near to him, after all the calamities of the church beyond the seas. But we grow worse and dishonor Him.[22]

Woe unto thee, O England!

This quickened tempo of the Jeremiad was a response to a purely religious stimulus—rising Anglicanism. But the content of the Jeremiad, from the very beginning, was not at all confined. We must keep in mind that the preachers were educated Englishmen as well as ministers, and so were subject to the same sense of discomfort emanating from the contrast of ideals and perceived reality which we have described. They were not alone among the ministers of England in this, certainly; the same discontent (and the same idealization of society) was reflected, for example, in their arch-nemesis, Laud when he wrote that "if any man be so addicted to his private, that he neglect the common, state, he is void of the sense of piety and wisheth peace and happiness to himself in vain."[23] But the preachers' discomfort with the purely religious course

---

22 Sermon of John Wilson, May 18, 1628, Keayne's Journal of John Cotton's English Sermons, 1620s, Massachusetts Historical Society.

23 William Scott and James Bliss, eds., *The Works of . . . William Laud* (London, 1847-60), I, 28-29.

of events exaggerated their discomfort as mere Englishmen. For them, God would spew his wrath upon England not merely for its irreligion or for that fall toward popery which they saw in the rise of Anglicanism but for the kingdom's fall from traditional ideals as well.[24]

In their sermons and pamphlets matters of doctrine, polity and faith were conjoined with an articulation and hallowing of social ideals. Thus Master William Perkins wrote of order: "God hath appointed that in every society one person should be above or under another; not making all equal as though the body should be all head and nothing else."[25] He linked, in another passage, organic unity with order, and order with diligence, fruitful labor, and sublimation of self (as did, it is worth remembering, the passage from the homilies and 1549 catechism quoted above): "That common saying, *Every man for himself, and God for us all*, is wicked and is directly against the end of every calling or honest kind of life."

In man's body there be sundry parts and members, and every one hath his several use and office, which it performeth not for itself, but for the good of the whole body; as the office of the eye, is to see, of the ear to hear, and the foot to go. Now all societies of men, are bodies, a family is a body, and so is every particular Church a body, and the common-wealth also: and in these bodies there be several members which are men walking in several callings and offices, the execution whereof, must tend to the happy and good estate of the rest. . . . God hath ordained and disposed all callings, and in his providence designed the persons to bear them. Here then we must in general know, that he abuseth his calling, whosoever he be that against the end thereof, employs it for himself, seeking wholly his own, and not the common good.[26]

---

[24] Perry Miller briefly alluded to the preachers' traditionalism (both in England and New England) in a typical sentence: "Springing from the traditions of the past, from the deep and wordless sense of the tribe, of the organic community, came a desire to intensify the social bond, to strengthen the cohesion of the folk." *The New England Mind: The Seventeenth Century* (New York, 1939), p. 440. In a sense this chapter is an exegesis of that verse.

[25] Quoted in Rutman, *Winthrop's Boston*, p. 11.

[26] In Morgan, ed., *Puritan Political Ideas*, p. 39.

Social phenomena were perceived and evaluated in terms of the traditional ideal—but with God firmly lodged on the side of the ideal. Thus preachers John Dod and Robert Cleaver wrote of "rogues and runagates who, being strong and lusty, make begging and wandering their trade of life": "What more dishonest thing can be in a Christian common-weal than that such men should be permitted? which fill the land with sin . . . that live without a calling, without magistracy, without ministry, without God in the world; that neither glorify God, nor serve the prince, nor profit the common-weal." Dod and Cleaver pointed to the changing status of the servant as well, a cause of the "rogues and runagates" but a social sin in and of itself:

> It is the custom of most men nowadays (so wretchedly covetous are they grown) that they toil their servants while they can labor, and consume their strength and spend them out: and then when age cometh, and the bones are full of ache and pain . . . they turn them out of the doors, poor and helpless into the wide world to shift for themselves as they can.

How very far such callousness was from the ideal—the ideal of Don Quixote and Sancho—was clear for "God chargeth the master of the family with all in the family . . . children, servants and inferiors whatsoever."[27]

Above all else this familial aspect of the ideal was stressed. The social role of the family was inherent in the ideal, and to the extent that the ideal was being hallowed, so too was the family. But to the extent that the family was charged with a particular and additional role in the preachers' evangelical mission, its place was exaggerated. A later minister put this additional role clearly when he advised his fellow ministers to "get masters of families to their duties, and they will spare you a great deal of labor with the rest, and further much the success of your labor. . . . You are like to see no general reformation till you procure family reformation."[28] Hence the preachers

---

[27] Quoted in Hill, *Society and Puritanism*, pp. 279, 284, 443.
[28] Richard Baxter, quoted in *ibid.*, p. 445.

asserted the family basis of society. Master Richard Greenham: "Of particular persons come families; of families, towns;
of towns, provinces; of provinces, whole realms."[29] Servant
and child alike—and with little distinction drawn between the
two—were commanded to subject themselves to the father, and
the father was commanded to deal justly and wisely with both.
The wife was commanded to accept her husband as he "on
whom God hath bestowed her, to whom he hath assigned
her."[30] And the preachers urged upon the family a "spirituali-
zation of the household," specifically, Bible-reading and family
prayers, family correction and discipline. "Let the master reform his servant, the father his child, the husband his wife."
"It belongs to all governors to see that their children, servants
and inferiors whatsoever keep the Lord's day." "If ever we
would have the church of God to continue among us, we must
bring it into our households and nourish it in our families."[31]

REFLECTIONS OF THE JEREMIAD: A CASE STUDY

A traditional idealization of society, violated to an apparent
degree by reality—so much might affect any Englishman
conscious of his social surroundings. The Jeremiad of the
preachers, increasing in tempo as Anglicanism rose, prophesy-
ing woe to England for its irreligion and falling toward popery
yet incorporating as a further sin the departure of England
from traditional social ideals and stressing the family as a social
and religious curative—so much should have a peculiar effect
upon the lay followers of the preachers accenting the Jeremiad. We should expect discomfort with the kingdom rising
in tune with the Jeremiad, discomfort enough perhaps to drive
some to seek refuge overseas. We should expect, too, that
with preachers putting God so stridently on the side of tradi-

[29] In Everett H. Emerson, *English Puritanism from John Hooper
to John Milton* (Durham, N.C., 1968), p. 153.
[30] Thomas Gataker, in *ibid.*, pp. 216-17.
[31] Hill, *Society and Puritanism*, pp. 443-45, quoting Edmund Calamy,
Dod and Cleaver, Greenham.

tional ideals, the lay followers' attachment to the ideals and their dismay at departures from them would be exaggerated over that of other Englishmen. Such a model seems borne out in the career and writing of John Winthrop.

We have already met Winthrop as a leader of the 1630 migration to New England. Born in the year of the Spanish Armada, a lawyer by profession and lord of the manor of Groton and of sundry other lands by gift and inheritance from his father, Winthrop was assuredly a lay Puritan, his association with the fellowship being clear. The association, equally clearly, had an effect upon Winthrop's religious outlook. He was awakened to a spiritual awareness as a young married man of about eighteen, the agent of his awakening being Master Ezekiel Culverwell, a friend and conferee of Cambridge's Chaderton and Wethersfield's Rogers. The agonizing quest which the preachers insisted was an obligation every man must undertake—that hard climb from the first realization of God's promises as put forth in the Bible to the tremulous hope that the grace won by Christ's sacrifice was imputed to oneself which has already been described—is accurately reflected in a journal kept by Winthrop at the time and in an account of his religious course prepared much later. Historian Edmund S. Morgan summarizes:

> After listening to Culverwell, Winthrop thought he could discern a change in his life. He gained a local reputation for piety, took to advising other people about their souls, and thought of entering the ministry. . . . Reading in Perkins and other Puritan writers, he discovered that a reprobate could do as much as he had, 'and now to hear others applaud me, was a dart through my liver'. But he still had not reached conviction. Instead of feeling the helplessness of his position, he redoubled his efforts to do good, and 'was brought to such bondage, as I durst not use my recreation, nor meddle with any worldly business, etc., for fear of breaking my peace.' Finally, at about the age of thirty (1618) God brought him to a true humiliation in which 'he laid me lower in mine own eyes than at any time before, and showed me the emptiness of all my gifts and parts, left me neither power nor will, so as I became as a weaned child.' With this, the work of preparation was

finally ended, and 'the good spirit of the Lord breathed upon
my soul, and said I should live.' There followed the expected
trials and temptations, but the spirit never wholly deserted
him: 'many falls I have had, and have lain long under some,
yet never quite forsaken of the lord.'[32]

In his quickened religious condition, Winthrop sought the
companionship of others similarly awakened. "I loved a Christian, and the very ground he went upon," he wrote. "I honored a faithful minister in my heart and could have kissed
his feet." He "had an insatiable thirst after the word of God
and could not miss a good sermon, though many miles off."[33]
The sermons, insofar as they accented the morphology of
conversion, drove Winthrop even deeper into introspection.
But insofar as they accented the Jeremiad they directed his
attention outward to the England about him, gradually imparting to him a sense of impending doom.[34]

This last we can trace in his writings. In 1622, in a letter to
a friend, we find reflected the preachers' mournful prophecy:
"The Lord look mercifully upon this sinful land, and turn us
to him by some repentance, otherwise we may fear it hath
seen the best days." Two years later he was involved in the
preparation of a list of "Common Grevances Groaninge for
Reformation." In the list were "Grevances" arising from the
growing pressure on the preachers: "the suspension and silencing of many painful learned ministers for not conformity in
some points of ceremonies," for example, and, by way of contrast, the many "scandalous and dumb [nonpreaching] ministers" left untouched by authority. But secular grievances
were prominent: inequities in the tax and legal structure, the
sad condition of England's poor.[35] The Lord was neither mer-
ciful nor were the grievances reformed, however, and as the
1620s advanced, as the Jeremiad increased in tempo, sacral and

[32] Morgan, *Visible Saints,* pp. 71-72. See also Morgan's brief biography, *The Puritan Dilemma: The Story of John Winthrop* (Boston and
Toronto, 1958).
[33] Massachusetts Historical Society, *Winthrop Papers,* I, 156.
[34] The substance of the "dilemma" of Morgan's title—see n. 32.
[35] Massachusetts Historical Society, *Winthrop Papers,* I, 268, 295 ff.

secular affairs—in Winthrop's eyes—degenerated. By May of 1629 his words reflected near-panic. These are "evil and declining times," he wrote from London to his wife at Groton:

> The increasing of our sins [as a people] gives us so great cause to look for some heavy scourge and judgment to be coming upon us: the Lord hath admonished, threatened, corrected and astonished us, yet we grow worse and worse, so as his spirit will not always strive with us, he must needs give way to his fury at last; he hath smited all the other [reformed] churches [of Europe] before our eyes, and hath made them to drink of the bitter cup of tribulation even unto death; . . . he is turning the cup toward us also, and because we are the last, our portion must be, to drink the very dregs which remain: my dear wife, I am verily persuaded, God will bring some heavy affliction upon this land, and that speedily.[36]

And when, a few months later, Winthrop outlined his reasons for leaving England, the sense of impending doom was again paramount. True, he put forth a positive argument for the New England venture: To carry "the gospel into those parts" and "to help raise and support a particular Church while it is in the bud and infancy" would be a service to God and of great use as an example to the godly everywhere. But bulking larger was a negative argument. England would no longer support her earnest Christians, he wrote. The kingdom has "grown to that height of intemperance as no man's estate will suffice him to keep sail with his equal and he that doth not must live in contempt"; its "trades are carried so deceitfully and unrighteously as it is almost impossible for a good upright man to maintain his charge and to live comfortably in his profession"; it groans "under her inhabitants so that man the best of creatures is held more base than the earth they tread on"; its people strive "for places of habitation." Here in England we meet "so many wandering ghosts in shape of men, so many spectacles of misery in all our streets, our houses full of victuals, and our entries full of hunger-starved Christians . . . our shops full of rich wares, and under our stalls lie our own flesh

---

[36] *Ibid.*, II, 91.

in nakedness. . . . All our towns complain of the burden of poor people and strive by all means to rid any such as they have, and to keep off such as would come to them." There, in New England, "whole countries useful and convenient for the use of men . . . lie waste without inhabitant." "All other [Protestant] churches of Europe being brought to desolation, it cannot be but that like judgement is coming upon us." And "who knoweth but that God hath prepared this place for a refuge for many whom he meaneth to save in the general destruction."[37]

Clearly in Winthrop we find reflected the rising tempo of the preachers' Jeremiad. He leaves England in 1630 in flight.[38] Traditionalism is reflected in Winthrop, too. He leaves in flight, but flight to what? One flees, obviously, to a situation free of those ills which precipitated flight—in Winthrop's case to an empty land in which he could attempt to build that degree of perfection which God would allow man. And aboard the *Arbella* carrying him to New England, Winthrop sketched social perfection as he envisioned it.[39] His conception should not be unfamiliar to us. Men, ideally, stood in seried ranks:

> God Almighty in his most holy and wise providence hath so disposed of the Condition of mankind, as in all times some must be rich, some poor, some high and eminent in power and dignity; others mean and in subjection.

The parts of society—by implication ranks, occupations, families, individuals—formed a single body and "being thus united"

---

[37] *Ibid.*, pp. 111-14, 122-23.

[38] Michael Walzer, *The Revolution of the Saints* (Cambridge, Mass., 1965), *passim*, postulates a number of responses to the discerned conditions in England. Lawrence Stone, "Social Mobility in England, 1500-1700," *Past & Present*, XXXIII (1966), 49, summarizes them: "Rigid self-discipline at the service of an ideology . . . cheerful opportunism, quietistic withdrawal and fierce nostalgia for a lost world." If these are not considered mutually exclusive, one can agree. Winthrop would seem to display both quietistic withdrawal and nostalgia.

[39] In his "A Modell of Christian Charity," Massachusetts Historical Society, *Winthrop Papers*, II, 282-95.

were "so contiguous in a special relation as they must needs partake of each other's strength and infirmity, joy and sorrow, weal and woe." Each part had its place and duty in the whole, and each accepted its place, diligently working for the good of the whole and taking its reward from the well-being of the whole. His simile was the human body and specifically the mouth which "is at all the pains to receive, and mince the food which serves for the nourishment of all the other parts of the body, yet it hath no cause to complain; for . . . the other parts send back by secret passages a due proportion of the same nourishment in a better form for the strengthening and comforting the mouth."

Thus far, Winthrop differed not one iota from thinking Englishmen everywhere. All defined the social ideal in such terms. But did not the preachers put God stridently on the side of the ideal? So too did Winthrop, and more! Social perfection was, for him, as much a gift from God as grace and salvation. For the achievement of the ideal was dependent upon man's perfect love for his brother, love being the "ligament" binding the parts in the single body. Adam, God's perfect creation, had the capability of perfect love, but in the aftermath of Adam's fall "every man is born with this principle in him, to love and seek himself only." And except that "Christ comes and takes possession of the soul," gathering together the scattered bones of "perfect old man Adam" and thereby re-engendering this capability for perfect love, society must—as it was so obviously in England—be imperfect. In this equating of perfect love, a product of God's grace, and perfect society, the Christian quest preached by the fellowship and the traditional idealization of society were hopelessly intertwined and the latter enormously exaggerated.

In New England, Disparate Reflections

Let us shift momentarily from old to New England, where an exaggerated and persistent traditionalism is found to be very much a mark of the society. The ordinances and actions of the first years of Massachusetts Bay display as much. Physical unity was enjoined by the initial settlement pattern, subsequently by a law requiring the settlers to build their houses within a half-mile of the meetinghouse; social unity was built around the family—servants being linked to families, families to land and church, ultimately to participation in community affairs—and protected by laws directed against "strangers" and unaffiliated laborers; the natural order of higher and lower, rulers and ruled, was inherent in the very institutions which allow us to identify a leadership, by the longevity in authority of the leaders, the relatively few challanges to them, and their responses to challenges; sublimation of self to the good of the community was evidenced in laws requiring fruitful labor, limiting wages, and setting prices. Historians studying specific New England towns have, for the early years, depicted societies startling for their resemblance to the traditional ideal of an interconnected and interdependent web of ordered families. And, most startling of all, historians have noted a longevity of tradition most readily demonstrated in secular rhetoric.[40] Thus Winthrop, in 1637, reflects the family orientation of society: "It is clearly agreed, by all, that the care of safety and welfare was the original cause or occasion of common weals and of many families subjecting themselves to rulers and laws. . . . A family is a little commonwealth, and a commonwealth is a great family." In the colonial records of Connecticut one finds declared in 1643 that "the prosperity and well being of Common Weals doth much depend upon the well government and ordering of particular families." The Massachusetts General Court in 1675 noted "a woeful breach of the fifth commandment to be found amongst us, in contempt of authority, civil, ecclesiastical, and domestical" and ordered the tightest enforcement of "the laws already made and provided in this case . . . and particularly that [regarding the] evil of inferiors absenting themselves out of the families

---

[40] See the general and local studies discussed in the appended bibliographical essay.

whereunto they belong." The same court noted the "sin of idleness," ordering constables to "inspect particular families, and present a list of the names of all idle persons." And in 1715, having information as to the "great deficiency in domestical or family government," the Assembly of Connecticut called for better "execution of those good laws already enacted amongst us, for the prevention of such decays."[41]

Unity, the ordered and organic nature of society, the mutual obligation of parts in society to each other and to the whole, the peaceful and harmonious meshing of parts, and the diligence of parts as each performs its appointed task—for all of these a similar chronological ordering of quotations could be put forth. And within one town after another the rhetoric can be demonstrated in reality. New England emerged from old England but, writes one historian, scholarship is tending to suggest "an ironic interpretation . . .: that it may, for a while at least, have been more 'traditional' in character than English society itself."[42]

Winthrop offers us a key to the relationship of this traditionalism to Puritanism. Recall that we have delimited Puritanism in terms of the preachers and conceptualized lay Puritanism as a gift from preachers to laymen—a gift which enters the lay mind not to sit solitary on the shelf but to mix and intermix with other elements, influencing action in a particular way and to a specific degree according to the condition of the recipient and the nature of the lay-preacher association. In Winthrop we can sense something of what the preachers might evoke in those who heard them hallow traditional values and prophesy the coming wrath of God toward England. But he was only one and New England was peopled

[41] Massachusetts Historical Society, *Winthrop Papers*, III, 423, 424; Nathaniel B. Shurtleff, ed., *Records of the Governor and Company of the Massachusetts Bay in New England* (Boston, 1853-54), V, 62; Arthur W. Calhoun, *A Social History of the American Family*, I, *Colonial Period* (University Paperbacks ed.; New York, 1960), p. 72; Bushman, *Puritan to Yankee*, p. 14.

[42] Philip J. Greven, Jr., "Historical Demography and Colonial America," *William and Mary Quarterly*, 3d ser., XXIV (1967), 453.

by thousands of Englishmen. To attempt to extrapolate from the one to the thousands would be foolhardy. Winthrop's reaction to the preachers' words was directly related to his condition and similar to the reaction of another only insofar as that other person's condition was similar to his. We need not reduce the logic of these considerations to absurdity and attempt to deal with each lay Puritan individually. However, we can and should categorize the hearers of the preachers and postulate, by categories, the effect of the preachers' words as their words might affect traditionalism. None has as yet attempted systematic categorization, but perhaps we can pioneer by suggesting three similar types of men.

First were those like Winthrop who might be expected to react in somewhat similar ways to the preachers' words. Winthrop was lord of the manor of Groton—country gentry. That he was also a lawyer was peripheral; as a London lawyer he was always desirous of returning home to be lord of the manor, a desire clear in Winthrop's letters to his wife.[43] As a group, the gentry had a recognized position within the ordered society. They were a part of the rural village, where at least a remnant of that older society, rationalized by traditional ideals, still existed—a point to which we will return. They knew at first hand, therefore, the reality of the ordered, functional society; indeed, they were at the apex of such a society within the villages, an enviable position. Too, they lived, in historian Lawrence Stone's words, under a "crushing burden of belief in the need for social stability" and resisted all change which was not put forth as "maintenance of tradition."[44] They were educated, the principal recipients of the expansion of education, hence knowledgeable of the rationalization of the traditional society. (Winthrop had spent two years at Cambridge.)

But if gentry such as Winthrop were familiar in theory and practice with traditional values, if they were conservative in

[43] Darrett B. Rutman, "My Beloved and good Husband . . .," *American Heritage*, XII (August, 1962), 24-27, 94-96.
[44] Stone, *Crisis of the Aristocracy*, p. 22.

their resistance to change which was not labeled traditional, they were in a position to sense departures from idealized tradition. Economically they were among the most exposed of Englishmen, as trade and market variations were reflected in the commodity prices and rents upon which they depended. Such exposure could only introduce insecurity, where the ideal implied an immutability for those of their rank and status. Similarly, they were among the most mobile of Englishmen. Winthrop, as he slowly rode back and forth between his London duties as attorney at the Court of Wards and Liveries and his rural duties as lord of Groton, surely was a first-hand witness to the poverty and beggary he inveighed against. Groton itself was on the boundary between two types of rural villages, and the very act of coming and going from Groton would show Winthrop diversity—here a nucleated, community-minded village; there a forest hamlet, the very opposite. And gentry such as Winthrop undoubtedly felt themselves alienated and suspicious of London, "the City," as England's leading class divided into "Country" and "Court." Lawrence Stone again: England was dividing into "two distinct cultures," the one adopted by the king, his courtiers, "by the majority of the nobility and a tiny handful of court gentry; the other by the majority of the gentry and a minority of country peers." In this division, "a belief in the virtues of country living" was being ranged "against the sophistication of the London man-about-town; a strong moral antipathy to sexual license, gambling, stage-plays, hard drinking, duelling, and running into debt, against a natural weakness for all these worldly pleasures and vices; a dark suspicion of ritual and ornament in church worship against a ready acceptance of the beauty of holiness advocated by Laud; and lastly a deeply felt fear and hatred of Papists and Popery against an easy-going toleration for well-connected recusants."[45]

Those of the "Country" who heard the preachers might find their staunch country morality strengthened, even if not per-

45 *Ibid.*, p. 502.

suaded to the preachers' doctrine. They might also equate England's sin, as the preachers pronounced it, with the "Court," hear that the Court was bringing down God's wrath, and that wrath would fall upon Country and Court alike. Given their mentality, it is not difficult to conceive of gentry other than Winthrop listening to the preachers and coming to somewhat the same conclusions as to impending wrath, flight, and the necessity for a revitalization of social values hallowed by the preachers. Certainly the leadership of "Puritan" colonization, not just in Massachusetts Bay but elsewhere in New England and in the Caribbean, came from just such gentlemen fearful of what lay ahead in England's future.[46] Certainly, too, those about the Earl of Lincoln's Tattershall household, as they considered the Massachusetts Bay venture in 1629 and 1630 independently of Winthrop, were thinking along much the same lines as he. Anne Bradstreet, writing in New England at a later date—as the English Civil War was breaking out—but undoubtedly reflecting the earlier attitude at Tattershall, personified old England and put into her mouth two revealing couplets:

> The sermons yet upon record do stand
> That cried destruction to my wicked land;
> I then believed not, now I feel and see,
> The plague of stubborn incredulity.

And in almost eerie duplication of Winthrop's letter to his wife of May, 1629 (that quoted above), the poetess has mother England continue:

> I saw sad Germany's dismantled walls.
> I saw her people famished, nobles slain,
> Her fruitful land, a barren heath remain.
> I saw, unmoved, her armies foiled and fled,
> Wives forced, babes tossed, her houses calcined.
> I saw strong Rochelle yielded to her foe,
> Thousands of starved Christians there also. . . .

---

[46] J. H. Hexter, *The Reign of King Pym* (Cambridge, Mass., 1941), pp. 77 ff.

Now sip I of that cup, and just 't may be
The bottom dregs reserved are for me.[47]

From the gentry at the apex of the village structure, turn to the generality of the countryside. For the purposes of envisioning England as those who discerned departures from the traditional idealization saw the kingdom, we earlier stressed the change and flux in the countryside. Now we must reverse ourselves. There was change. This we must concede unless we are prepared to argue, among other things, that the critics were deluding themselves completely. But there was a traditional reality as well. Indeed, life was lived in England far more in the context of the social ideal we have called traditional than it was in anything approaching a modern ideal. Writes one historian: "With infinite local variation in detail" and in spite of changes, the countryside "was still characterized by a certain unity of outlook, and that unity was based, in the main, on distinctly peasant preconceptions."[48]

The key word is "peasant," a state of mind rather than a social or economic status. The peasant mentality has a tenacious attachment to the land and beasts by which life is maintained, to family and the strength of family ties, and to the web of families making up the village. It delights in the known relationship and is suspicious of any breaches or changes. It values conformity and seeks always to enforce a single mode of behavior. It clings to tradition, even in the ways of work, which "must be the regular sort to which [the peasant] is accustomed, which he did beside his father as a boy, which *his* father did, and *his* father before him; the same old plough or grub-axe, the same milking, the same identical mowing, if possible in the same field. He does not care for any new-

---

[47] "A Dialogue Between Old England and New," lines 132-35, 143-49, 153-55, in Jeannine Hensley, ed., *The Works of Anne Bradstreet* (Cambridge, Mass., 1967). Mistress Bradstreet was the daughter of one and the wife of another of the Earl's stewards; both father and husband would serve as governors of Massachusetts Bay.

[48] Alan Everitt in Finberg, ed., *The Agrarian History of England and Wales*, IV, 454.

fangled jobs. He does not recognize them, they have no *locus standi*—they are not established."[49] The peasant community— the English village of the early seventeenth century—does not articulate its values. It simply lives by them. But we would not be far wrong if we set those values down in the familiar words unity, order, the family structure of society, diligence, and a subsuming of self to the good of the whole.[50]

Delivered in the village setting to men of peasant mentality, what might the preachers' words evoke? In terms of religion, perhaps a great deal. A villager, as well as a Winthrop, might be awakened to the Christian quest. And ultimately, if his preacher was forced from the pulpit by a bishop, if the preacher took ship for New England, if the zeal for the preacher and the Christian quest were strong enough, and if New England was put forth in ardent enough terms as a New Jerusalem, the villager might leave the known for the unknown. Too, the Jeremiad might frighten the villager. To the farmer, God's wrath can assume a very personal and immediate form—too much or too little rain, locusts, crop failures, and attendant famine. Perhaps fright might force the villager from his village and toward New England.

But what of the articulation of traditional social values by the preacher? One suggests that the villager well settled in known surroundings, living a traditional life, needs no such articulation. To tell such a man that society must be knit together as one family is to articulate the obvious. He will not rush off to find such a society when he has one already. But if the villager was divorced from known surroundings (whatever the reason) we can postulate that he would feel discomfort, uneasiness, a desire to reestablish himself in a known system of relationships. To the extent that there was flux and movement in the English countryside, that men moved from one village to another in search of the main chance—to that

[49] *Ibid.*, p. 434.
[50] See in general Eric R. Wolf's brief *Peasants* (Englewood Cliffs, N.J., 1966) and Robert Redfield's *Peasant Society and Culture* (Chicago, 1966).

extent we can postulate discomfort in the peasant mind and an attraction to the preachers' articulation of old values. And certainly, no matter what the motivation which sends the villager to New England, be it the search for a New Jerusalem, or fear, or simply the possibility for economic advancement in New England—land!—the villager, with his peasant mentality, would strive to encapsulate himself in a village community such as he had left behind. Such a man would then desperately need (and heed) the articulation of traditional social values, if only as a guide.

In Puritan studies, our third category is classic—the townsman, the urban "middle class." The equating of Protestantism with "rising capitalism," Puritanism with left Protestantism, hence Puritanism with such "rising capitalism" is common and, when so simply put, fallacious. The preachers had their following in the towns and in London. But far from practitioners of any new ways in business or commerce, the preachers' followers within the towns tended in the main to be artisans and small businessmen, some prospering, some not, but all feeling themselves threatened by what they discerned as new ways; men and women who had left the village reality and, immensely alone with a mentality which eschewed aloneness, frightened, found solace in the preachers.[51] The preachers' articulation of tradition was a proferred antidote to all of the real and perceived breaches of tradition which were disturbing or threatening. The doctrine of the preachers, moreover, gave expression to feelings of "insignificance and powerlessness" brought on by the unfamiliar size and impersonality of town or city. Doctrine, too, rationalized those feelings to the extent that insignificance and powerlessness were put forth as steps on the road to grace. And finally, insofar as the preachers inveighed against immorality (broadly defined) and separated the godly from the ungodly, Christian from non-Christian— either in mere words or by actually gathering questing Chris-

---

[51] Erich Fromm, *Escape from Freedom* (Discus Books ed.; New York, 1965), pp. 81-122.

tians about them—so far did the preachers offer a new "village" community, albeit within a town or city, for those who felt the lack. Indeed, the preachers' town followers were almost unique in their responsiveness to the preachers' gatherings. Gentry, with an established position in society, had little felt-need to find a position in such a substitute society—Winthrop, for example, cannot be linked to a gathering; Anne Bradstreet, representative of the Tattershall group, had a difficult time adjusting to the gatherings instituted in New England as the church.[52] The rural villagers, too—by definition—had a known position in society and so felt little pull toward the gatherings. But the very propensity for the gathering which the townsmen had to an exceptional degree is indicative of their propensity for a traditional structuring of society for which, to some extent at least, the gathering was a replacement.

Gentry, villagers, townsmen—we can conceive of each hearing the preachers in a given way. Yet we must make clear that within each group there were undoubtedly those who were *not* hearers of the preachers; that there were, moreover, gentry, villagers, and townsmen who, while they might have heard the preachers and reacted as we have suggested, might have heard and/or reacted to a lesser, even minimal degree. If, therefore, we are to categorize those who took ship to New England (rather than the hearers of the preachers) we would have to add a fourth category: those of our previous three categories who were not particularly influenced by the preachers. Such would bring with them to New England the traditionalism of their category less only the special slant or exaggeration which the preachers imparted.

TRADITION AND COUNTER-TRADITION IN NEW ENGLAND

From the various parts of England and from each of our groups—plus the fourth group of those relative strangers to the preachers and Puritanism—came the New Englanders. A few

---

[52] Hensley, ed., *Works of Anne Bradstreet*, p. ix.

had arrived before Winthrop; 700 arrived with him; 20,000 arrived in the first decade. We can conjecture that they came, as has been peripherally suggested in regard to the villagers, for a variety of motives. Some followed prominent lay leaders; over a hundred came from the immediate vicinity of Winthrop's Groton in 1630. Some followed a particular preacher, as Anne Hutchinson did. An ardent follower of Master Cotton, she seized upon the promise of a verse from Isaiah—"Thine eyes shall see thy teachers"—and traveled after Cotton when he left old England for New.[53] Some came in search of a New Jerusalem. And some came merely in pursuit of the main chance. Scattered in villages around Boston Bay, at the base of Cape Ann, soon along the Connecticut River valley and Long Island Sound, they created in short order a traditional reality. Men who sought God and men who sought the main chance alike had an innate thrust toward such a creation, but to the degree that the settlers were followers of the preachers, the thrust was exaggerated. And that there were men who were consciously intent on such a creation, who envisioned a revitalization of traditional values—lay leaders like Winthrop and the preachers themselves—made the creation all the easier.

In the settlement of Dedham in Massachusetts we can, perhaps, discern this course.[54] Unity, order, the family structure of society, diligence, and sublimation of self—these values were inherent in the thirty-odd families which would begin the town in 1636, part of their English culture in general and in varying kind and degree among the families exaggerated to the extent each had heard the sermons of the preachers. As culture, such values were as much packed and carried from old England to

---

[53] Emery Battis, *Saints and Sectaries: Anne Hutchinson and the Antinomian Controversy in the Massachusetts Bay Colony* (Chapel Hill, N.C., 1962), chap. V.

[54] I have been privileged to read in manuscript form Kenneth A. Lockridge's *A New England Town: The First Hundred Years* (New York, 1970). My debt to Professor Lockridge is very great, but I must make clear that in this particular respect I have gone beyond his study in applying my conceptualizations to his Dedham.

New as the material baggage of clothes and tools packed into the holds of the ships carrying the families. But on arrival the families were strangers to the land and to each other. The values evoked felt-needs rather than reflected a reality. Each family individually felt discomfited in the absence of a sense of unity, of conjunction with other families in some common endeavor. They sought satisfaction of their need within the institutional framework established by the lay leaders, coming together as a single body and petitioning the Massachusetts General Court for a tract of land upon which to seat themselves as a town. From the ministers they took the notion of convenant, in part to form a covenanted gathering as their church, but in part to articulate their intentions to establish themselves as a traditional community by writing a town covenant:[55]

> We whose names are here unto subscribed do, in the fear and reverence of our Almighty God, mutually and severally promise amongst ourselves and each other to profess and practise one truth according to that most perfect rule, the foundation whereof is everlasting love. . . . That we shall by all means labor to keep off from us all such as are contrary minded. . . . That if at any time difference shall arise between parties of our said town, that then such party and parties shall presently refer all such difference unto some one, two, or three others of our said society to be fully accorded and determined. . . . That every man that . . . shall have lots in our said town shall pay his share in all [charges] . . . as also become freely subject unto all such orders and constitutions as shall be . . . made now or at any time hereafter from this day forward, as well for loving and comfortable society in our said town as also for the prosperous and thriving condition of our said fellowship. . . . And for the better manifestation of our true resolution herein,

---

[55] Notably Winthrop did as much when, in the "Modell of Christian Charity," he invoked the notion of a covenant to bind together as a social body settlers who were strangers to each other: "Though we were absent from each other many miles, and had our employments as far distant, yet we ought to account our selves knit together. . . . Thus stands the cause between God and us, we are entered into Covenant with him for this work." Massachusetts Historical Society, *Winthrop Papers*, II, 292, 294.

every man so received [into the town is] to subscribe hereunto his name, thereby obliging both himself and his successors after him for ever, as we have done.[56]

And finally, from their memory of how things were done in the villages at home they took the mundane components of their new village: the shape and appearance of the houses to be built and the placement of houses; the way land was to be divided among the villagers; the old village traditions, now written into town ordinances, which regulated men's relations to each other with regard to crops, cattle (who should reimburse whom when one man's cow strayed into another man's corn), the laying out and maintaining of streets and fences, morality. Very quickly Dedham became as English as one could possibly hope to make it in the new environment, and as traditional. No longer strangers to each other, the Dedham families were comfortably ensconced in a familiar and unitary social web.

But if traditionalism came to New England, so did the anti-thesis—that flux and change which in England appeared so at odds with the traditional idealization of society. Few who read the records of the New England colonies will not be struck by the redundant expostulations of laymen, ministers, and laws *against* violations of the traditional ideal; indeed, the prevalence of those ideals is most easily demonstrated by quoting tirades against violations, and it hardly seems likely that tirades would have been delivered in the absence of violations.

Diligence in some was matched by sloth in others. Some servants wanted no part of family discipline, and some masters of families nothing of servants but their labor. The ordered nature of society was at times violated by an unseemly desire for upward mobility, for an improved political status to match an improved economic status. Sublimation of self to society was matched by exaltation of self in pursuit of personal gain. Thus, men who left their old English village for New England

---

[56] Don Gleason Hill *et al.*, eds., *Early Records of the Town of Dedham* (Dedham, Mass., 1886-1936), III, 2-3.

in search of profit (as some most certainly did) initially might seek the comfort of a recreated traditional village, sublimating themselves to the new community in order to gain the comfort it offered, but the same urge which brought them to abandon what they had in England could lead them to abandon what they were creating in New England. Even those motivated to cross the ocean less by profit and more by religion (and hence more wedded to the traditional by the preachers' rhetoric) could be tempted away from the village by the promise of profit. In both cases the physical and social unity of the traditional village would be broken. Men remaining within a single village sometimes put themselves above the community. Merchant Robert Keayne would do so all unconsciously in Boston. Ironically, the preachers' doctrine itself led in this direction, for while they spoke to what one writer has called "the human needs of the frightened, uprooted, and isolated individual who had to orient and to relate himself to a new world [order]," some of the very qualities which they urged —"compulsion to work, passion for thrift, the readiness to make one's life a tool for the purpose of an extra personal power, asceticism, and a compulsive sense of duty"—were traits conducive to personal aggrandizement.[57] Unity, moreover, was sometimes shattered by argument, a tendency inherent in the nature of the emigration, involving as it did so many people from so many areas of old England. Men from different parts of England came with different memories of how things were done before and argued as to which memory should guide the new community (this happened in Sudbury, Massachusetts); or men from various parts of England grouped themselves by point of origin and argued for preeminence in the community (this in Hingham).[58]

---

[57] Fromm, *Escape from Freedom*, pp. 121-22. For Keayne's case see Bernard Bailyn, ed., *The Apologia of Robert Keayne: The Self-Portrait of a Puritan Merchant* (Harper Torchbooks ed.; New York, 1965).

[58] Powell, *Puritan Village*, chap. VIII; John J. Waters, "Hingham, Massachusetts, 1631-1661: An East Anglian Oligarchy in the New World," *Journal of Social History,* I (1967-68), 351-70.

The antithesis of traditional values worked its will most obviously at the center—in Boston—as that town grew so quickly from village to city. Size alone worked against tradition, sheer population growth forcing the division of men, where tradition accented unity. Men living in different geographic parts of the town, for example, divided their loyalties between the part and the whole; the one church formed originally could not physically accommodate all, hence a second, then a third church had to be organized, dividing men's loyalties between a particular church and the town in general. The town's turn to trade and commerce, most notably after 1640, enhanced a drive for personal gain, created occupational diversity (and on the basis of occupation men divided their loyalties still again), augmented the number of laborers unattached to families, and attracted men to the community from the Atlantic world of commerce who had no commitment to the town or society, only a commitment to themselves.[59]

Beyond Boston, however, tradition—at least on the surface —held strong, even to the extent of an institutionalization within a traditional framework of counter-traditional impulses. Thus, for example, as men tended in any given town to disperse to scattered farmsteads from an initially compact village center, the agencies of the village were stretched to accommodate the scattering; townsmen settling too far for even the stretched community to encompass regularly encapsulated themselves anew by forming a new town and seceding from the old. To note another example, arbitration and compromise, both within and between communities, in the interest of unity became so fundamental to the society as to subsume most conflict (yet at the same time making what conflict there was stand out in sharp relief). Within communities and individual families, too, a delicate balance was constructed between the unity of the family under the father and the desire of sons for land, families of their own, and status—a balance increasingly

---

[59] Rutman, *Winthrop's Boston, passim.*

threatened as one generation begat another, population rose, and the amount of available land within a given town shrank.[60]

Ultimately, of course, the tensions between tradition and counter-tradition could be accommodated nowhere. The traditional gave way—social unity to the institutionalization of diversity and conflict (the politics of representative democracy) and to geographic mobility ("frontier" restlessness or, more apt if less exciting, urban restlessness as men sought livelihoods apart from the land altogether); sublimation of self to exaltation of self (individualism); order to a veneration of social mobility (equalitarianism with its "rags to riches," "poor boy to president" mythology); the family structure of society to the interest structure of society and the family's isolation.

Historians studying New England have more often than not depicted the shift as beginning as the seventeenth century gave way to the eighteenth. Pointing to the country towns, to the compromise of conflict, to the stretching of the tradiional framework, to the strength of the family, above all to the pervasiveness of a traditional rhetoric, they have drawn a word-picture of a static, traditional, unchanging seventeenth-century society giving way in a rush at century's end to the broad trends which would produce our modern world. Other historians, pointing to Boston, to the here and there conflict in which men pushed themselves and their desires to the point of violating traditional mores, to the counter-traditional forces which lay behind the stretching of a traditional framework, have depicted an imperfect traditionalism from the very beginning and the gradual disintegration throughout the seven-

---

[60] Bushman, *Puritan to Yankee*, pt. 1; Michael Zuckerman, "The Massachusetts Town in the Eighteenth Century" (unpublished Ph.D. dissertation, Harvard University, 1967), *passim; idem,* "The Puritan Concept of Local History: An Exercise in Anachronism," paper delivered at the 28th annual meeting of the American Association for State and Local History, Washington, D.C., September, 1968—my gratitude to Professor Zuckerman for allowing me a copy; Greven, "Family Structure in Seventeenth-Century Andover," pp. 234-56; Kenneth A. Lockridge, "Land, Population and the Evolution of New England Society, 1630-1790," *Past & Present,* XXXIX (1968), 62-80.

teenth century of whatever there was of it.[61] The two views are not irreconcilable, for in the century both tradition and counter-tradition were at work in New England. The historian will discern whichever he looks for, although ideally he will look for both.

The prevalence of a traditional reality is, nevertheless, the most striking characteristic of seventeeth-century New England for those who are interested in Puritanism and the Christian fellowship which, in our conceptualization, imparts meaning to that term. The nature of the Winthrop venture itself gave the impetus to this long-lived traditionalism, for Winthrop's ideals were a guiding influence in the very first years. We have already postulated the relationship between those ideals and the preachers of the fellowship. The phenomenon noted at the end of the last chapter cemented and prolonged traditionalism: the coming of the preachers in great numbers relative to the population, seventy-seven in the years to roughly 1640, one practicing minister for every 415 people in the Massachusetts of 1650. Deferred to for their learning, their godliness, and their status as ministers, dispersed in pulpits in just about every town, all but monopolizing communication and education in New England—they were in effect the radio, television, newspaper, magazine, schoolteacher, erudite professor, and Fourth-of-July orator of that time and place— the ministers put forth in more vigorous terms than even in England the traditional values.

In England the ministers had equated the traditional with godliness and what they discerned as counter-traditional with sin, but only as part of a Jeremiad evoked by a particular religious situation. Their social comment was little more than a minor theme in a rich symphony built around the strictly religious—albeit lay hearers such as Winthrop, with lay concerns more paramount, reacted to the minor theme in a major way. In New England, however, a New England discerned as a new

---

.61 E.g., Bushman, *Puritan to Yankee*, on the one hand and Rutman, *Winthrop's Boston*, on the other.

beginning, God-inspired, certainly attuned to God (or at least God's message via the preachers), society was to be built anew in a godly form. The social content of the Jeremiad—the espousal of traditional values and the condemnation of departures from tradition—emerged from a minor into a major theme. The refrain is familiar: unity, order, the family structure of society, diligence, sublimation of self to the community. And being ministers of the Gospel in a God-fearing age, the ministers framed their proscriptions and prescriptions as commands from God given to men in Holy Writ. A God-fearing New England populace (already tending for a variety of reasons toward the traditional when subjected to this ministerial barrage) was perforce influenced by it. Not all New Englanders had been children of the fellowship in old England, certainly; and those associated with the fellowship in England had been associated to different degrees and different effect. But in New England all were children of tradition, born to it by their English origins and the very act of migration, held to it by the augmented traditionalism of the fellowship that lived with them. Wherever traditional values and their antithesis were in confrontation, wherever men were pulled one way by old values and another by new opportunities or new ways, the ministerial voice weighted the case. The wonder is not that New England clung to traditional values to the extent and for as long as the section did, but that there was any tendency at all to depart from tradition.

CHAPTER 4

THE FELLOWSHIP IN THE WILDERNESS

NEW ENGLAND RELIGIOSITY: THE ESSENTIAL DISTINCTIONS

Religion was, of course, the major motivation and central concern of the Christian fellowship of ardent preachers by which we have delimited Puritanism. Traditionalism was but a minor element of their Jeremiad in England, important for its impact upon some lay minds (Winthrop's, for example), vital insofar as it contributed to imparting and maintaining a particular form to New England society. But, in a sense, our exploration of traditionalism has been in the nature of an excursion along a country byway. It is time to return to the main thoroughfare, to the ministerial commitment to preaching and the cure of souls, to converting individuals from mere life to the life of Christian quest, in a word, to piety, and carry this commitment from old England to New.

As we make this turn back to the highroad, we must point our direction clearly by stipulating two essential ideas.

First, the ministers of the fellowship had not one but two primary commitments. If, on the one hand, the fellowship was one of evangelists committed to awakening piety (the essential Puritan commitment as we have defined it), its members were, on the other, ministers of the Gospel, hence members of a broader profession, and committed to the values of that profession. Certainly the preachers differed in beliefs from ministers tending toward an Anglican persuasion. But we too frequently accent the differences to the neglect of similarities. The preachers were products of the same university training as their antagonists and were molded by the same structured fabric of church life which they, as well as their antagonists, had aspired to enter as students and did enter as young men—albeit seeking its reform. As ministers, the preachers were committed to the institutionalization of religion (a formal church); within that church, whatever form they would have it assume, they valued authority, discipline, and unity. They were, as ministers, committed to bringing God's one and only truth to the world and to the church, although they might argue as to which was the right truth. And they had a common image of their role within church and society and of the respect toward their persons which the role demanded. They were, in their own eyes at least, the shepherds of the flock, the academicians of the Lord, and, in the separate but coordinate division of society into church and state, the proper administrators of the former.[1]

The point to be noted here is that these ministerial commitments and the Puritan commitment were not necessarily compatible. The effort to awaken each man to an individual quest tends actually to deny the institutionalization of religion and the monopolization of religious administration and teaching by the ministers, for the quest need not necessarily be carried on within the formal bounds of a church (however that church might be organized) or under the tutelage of one of God's official shepherds. As historian Alan Simpson has remarked, the basic Puritan impulse leads easily to the idea of the "individual as a church in himself" and to "prophetic scorn against the notion that ecclesiastical or civil coercion

---

[1] See Winthrop S. Hudson, "The Ministry in the Puritan Age," in H. Richard Niebuhr and Daniel D. Williams, eds., *The Ministry in Historical Perspectives* (New York, 1956), pp. 180-206.

can contribute anything to the growth of grace."[2] To put the matter succinctly, the preacher as an evangelist tended to unleash on men the Holy Spirit; the preacher as a minister tended to confine the Spirit in an institution dominated by himself. This incompatibility of basic commitments was of little importance in England; it was to be of vast importance in New England.

We must stipulate, secondly, that the ministerial call for conversion, for leaving the life of mere man and embarking on the Christian quest, was of a nature quite separate from the lay response to such a call. Each of the two—call and response —took place in a different setting. The fellowship enunciated the call within a broad theological setting, one more and more exclusively its own as Anglicanism evolved and left Calvinism to the fellowship. The layman, whether or not he understood the theology, received and responded to the call in what we can term a psychosocial setting—a phrase to be clarified later.

Within the context of these two ideas—that the commitment of the preachers was twofold and schizophrenic; that the preacher's call for conversion and the layman's response were of two different natures—New England's religious course can be considered in terms of four elements, only the first and third of which are here construed as peculiarly Puritan: The preachers' commitment to awakening men to the Christian quest; the ministerial commitment to an institutional church; a theological morphology of conversion; the timeless nature of man and the nature of society in which men of that time and place lived.

Puritan and Ministerial Commitments

It is not difficult to sketch for New England the overt results of the fellowship's incompatible commitments. As ministers of the fellowship arrived in New England in and immediately after 1630, they took advantage of the absence of any ecclesi-

---

[2] Alan Simpson, *Puritanism in Old and New England* (Chicago, 1955), p. 44.

astical limitations upon their preaching—New England's "wide door of liberty," Perry Miller called it[3]—to fulfill the Puritan values of the fellowship. They preached often, openly, and without reservations, each in his own fashion drawing men to God. And given the susceptibility of the laymen (a susceptibility, as we shall see, inherent in the social situation), the ministers were enormously successful.

In Boston, John Cotton's sermons provoked an ardor amazing even to Winthrop:

> More were converted and added to that church, than to all the other churches in the bay. . . . Divers profane and notorious evil persons came and confessed their sins, and were comfortably received into the bosom of the church. Yea, the Lord gave witness to the exercise of prophecy, so as thereby some were converted, and others much edified.[4]

At Salem, Roger Williams held forth for a while—that *enfant terrible* of seventeenth-century New England, a windmill gone mad as another New Englander described him, a minister in whom the ministerial values were completely overweighed by the Puritan. Asked at one time by Winthrop what he sought, Williams answered that he searched for "Jesus who was nailed to the gallows," asked "the way to lost Zion," and longed "for the bright appearance of the Lord Jesus to consume the man of sin."[5] In 1634 in Salem the "king's colors" were defaced on the grounds that its "red cross was given to the king of England by the pope, as an ensign of victory, and so a superstitious thing, and a relic of antichrist." In Dorchester, in April of 1636, would-be members of a new church were found to have "builded their comfort of salvation" upon "dreams and ravishes of spirit by fits; others upon the reformation of their lives; others upon duties and performances." And, climactically,

---

[3] In *Orthodoxy in Massachusetts, 1630-1650* (Cambridge, Mass., 1933), chap. V.

[4] James Kendall Hosmer, ed., *Winthrop's Journal "History of New England," 1630-1649* (New York, 1908), I, 116.

[5] Perry Miller, *Roger Williams: His Contribution to the American Tradition* (Atheneum ed.; New York, 1962), p. 47.

in Boston in 1636 and 1637 Cotton's preaching provoked among
his listeners what has been called the antinomian movement, as
a majority of the church, led by Anne Hutchinson, sought
(and some found) assurance of election in a perfect merger
of their flesh and Christ's spirit, holding that the personal dis-
covery of the spirit within was the only "infallible certain
evidence of our Justified estate."[6]

The ministerial commitment is as readily discernible. Religiosity, a sense that a religious institution was essential within
any society, and the familiarity of some of the first preachers
and settlers with the gatherings of questing Christians in old
England had inspired and imparted form to the first churches
of New England. The professedly godly among the leading
settlers of any particular town had simply come together as a
covenanted gathering, admitted others after testing their godliness, appointed officers, including preachers, and united with
the covenanted gatherings of other towns out of a general
sense of the desirability of unity.[7]

This sense of unity had arrived in New England even before
the Winthrop group, the lay leaders of Salem writing to Plymouth in 1629 of "God's people" being "marked with one and
the same mark, and sealed with one and the same seal, and
[having] for the main one and the same heart, guided by one
and the same spirit of truth."[8] It was reflected in and immediately after 1630 in correspondence and conferences between
the various gatherings as they faced common problems, in public lectures which brought men and women from many
gatherings together, and in the very early custom of existing
gatherings sending delegates to witness the formation of a new

------

[6] Hosmer, ed., *Winthrop's Journal*, I, 137, 177; Massachusetts Historical
Society, *Winthrop Papers*, III, 326. See also James F. Maclear, " 'The
Heart of New England Rent': The Mystical Element in Early Puritan
History," *Mississippi Valley Historical Review*, XLII (1956), 621-52.

[7] Rutman, *Winthrop's Boston*, pp. 47 ff., 283 ff. Note that the fact of
different degrees of familiarity with the gatherings was reflected in arguments over the form of the church that first year.

[8] "Governor [William] Bradford's Letter Book," Massachusetts Historical Society, *Collections*, 1st ser., III (1794), 66.

gathering and offering to it "the right hand of fellowship." With the appearance of the ministerial fellowship in significant numbers in 1632 and 1633, however, this vague union hardened rapidly into a firm institution.

Living and preaching in close proximity in New England—as they had not been in old England—and prone to travel about, listening to each other's doctrines as they were delivered in Sabbath sermons and weekday lectures, the newly arrived ministers noted differences in the details of their doctrines and were disturbed. But more: All about them gatherings were being formed as churches, and the transmutation of the English gathering into a New England church was thrusting questions before the ministers. As they had not been in England, the ministers found themselves drawn into a meaningful (rather than merely abstract) consideration of the proper form and structure of the church. Who was to be admitted and who refused? What were the proper officers of the church, and what was their proper relationship to the congregation? How were the churches to maintain communion with one another in that unity which all—ministers and laymen—felt was so important? Individually, the ministers were arriving at different answers. Laymen within the churches were offering still other answers. All this was in violation of the preachers' ministerial commitment to unity of doctrine (including the notion of God's single truth to be reflected in every church), to order under the aegis of their own authority, and to discipline. Very quickly the ministers turned to their fellowship in order to discern truth, reinstituting the primary mechanism of the English fellowship in New England—the ministerial meeting.

The first hint of such is found in 1633, when, following the arrival of Masters Thomas Hooker and John Cotton, considered by all as paramount members of the English fellowship, John Winthrop noted that "the ministers in the bay" area began meeting "once a fortnight, at one of their houses by course, where some question of moment was debated." The sort of questions discussed is indicated by the fears of a few who complained that such meetings "might grow in time

to a presbytery or superintendency, to the prejudice of the churches' liberties."[9] In 1635, in the process of rationalizing the banishment of Roger Williams, the ministers drew up "A Model of Church and Civil Power," an ecclesiastical constitution based upon theories of church government discussed publicly and privately in England since the late 1590s. God, the ministers wrote, "hath given a distinct power to *Church* and *Common-weal,* the one *Spiritual* (called the Power of the *Keys*) the other *Civil* (called the Power of the *Sword*)." "The common and last end of both is God's glory, and Man's eternal felicity." The leaders of the commonwealth must be the "nursing fathers" of the church, defending "the pure worship of God" with "the power of the sword against all those who shall attempt to corrupt it." Yet they must leave to the ministers the definition of "the pure worship of God." "In corrupt times" the commonwealth was to call "those who are most fit in several Churches"—and who are more fit for the work than the ministers?—"to assemble together in a Synod, to discuss and declare from the Word of God [the Bible], matters of Doctrine and Worship, and to help forward the Reformation of the Churches [of] God"; "in reformed times" —implicitly the normal times of New England—the commonwealth was to give "Liberty to the Elders [ministers] of several Churches to assemble themselves by their own mutual and voluntary agreement, at convenient times, as the means appointed by God, whereby he may mediately reform matters amiss in churches."[10] Between 1633 and 1636, too, the ministers as a body assumed authority over the establishment of new churches, an authority formalized in the "Model" and by law in Massachusetts Bay in the latter year. "The right hand

---

[9] Hosmer, ed., *Winthrop's Journal,* I, 112-13.

[10] The "Model," described as "composed by Mr. Cotton and the Ministers of New England," is interspersed in Roger Williams' *The Bloudy Tenent, of Persecution, for Cause of Conscience* (1644), in Reuben Aldridge Guild *et al.,* eds., *The Complete Writings of Roger Williams* (New York, 1963), III, 220-413. A portion is extant as an undated, untitled fragment in the library of the American Antiquarian Society, Worcester, Mass. The quotations are from pp. 222, 226, 232, 312, 390-91.

of fellowship" voluntarily proferred by an existing church and accepted by a new church was transformed into a ministerial hand, and that it be proferred as a sign of approbation of the new church by the ministry was decreed as mandatory. In 1637 a synodical precedent was laid down, as the ministers met publicly to condemn eighty-two doctrinal errors and nine "unsafe speeches" prevalent in the commonwealth.[11] Thereafter, in synods and councils, in their coming together to approve the gatherings of new churches, and in their private meetings, the ministers regularly acted as a corporate authority in the religious life of New England. Their synods were landmarks in the ecclesiastical history of New England.[12] Their councils—formal and public gatherings usually called to settle internal differences within a single church—were lesser landmarks. But in the day-to-day affairs of the churches of Christ, their private and less dramatic meetings were the most important.

We know little of these ministerial meetings. No formal records were kept, and they are discernible only now and again in public records, private journals, diaries, letters, travel accounts, and local church records. They were, apparently, geographically oriented, as the meetings of the fellowship in old England had been, the ministers of a given locality gathering periodically. But only the meetings in the immediate area of Boston have been systematically studied,[13] although there is every indication of similar meetings elsewhere in the Bay commonwealth, in Plymouth colony, and in Connecticut. More than 160 such meetings have been separately identified

---

[11] Shurtleff, ed., *Records of the Governor and Company of the Massachusetts Bay*, I, 168; David D. Hall, ed., *The Antinomian Controversy, 1636-1638: A Documentary History* (Middletown, Conn., 1968), pp. 219 ff.

[12] See the major synodical documents in Williston Walker, ed., *The Creeds and Platforms of Congregationalism* (Pilgrim Press ed.; Boston, 1960).

[13] By Robert Francis Scholz in his " 'The Reverend Elders': Faith, Fellowship and Politics in the Ministerial Community of Massachusetts Bay, 1630-1710" (unpublished Ph.D. dissertation, University of Minnesota, 1966).

between 1633 and 1672 in the Boston area alone, and even this number seems only a part of a much larger number. Cotton Mather wrote late in the century of "frequent meetings" by the ministers, "most usually after their public and weekly or monthly lectures, wherein they consulted for the welfare of their churches"; Robert Keayne, in the mid-1650s, made provision in his will for refreshments and a room for meetings in the Boston Town House, observing that the neighboring ministers met monthly, "chiefly in summer time," in order "to confer about ordering things in the churches" and debate "about doubts or difficult questions." Frequently the ministers in their meetings were called upon for (or volunteered) advice on public policy. But it is with church affairs that we are concerned. The assembled ministers considered such problems as the financial support of the ministry and the supplying of ministers to leaderless congregations. They advised individual churches on matters of polity and doctrine, even individual ministers about what not to preach. They conciliated differences within churches, admonished church members, whole churches, even fellow ministers found to be in error, and prepared a defense of the evolving New England religious system against critics in New England and old. In brief, the corporate body of the ministry—or, in the parlance of the time, the "reverend Elders" of New England—were in practice and in their writings constructing a peculiar church government.[14]

ARDOR, INSTITUTIONS, AND THEOLOGY

If it is not difficult to sketch in such fashion the emanations of the Puritan and ministerial drives—that of the former being an outpouring of religious ardor, and of the latter a firm religious institution—the sketch is nevertheless not enough. It

---

[14] Mather, *Magnalia Christi Americana*, I, 241-42; Bailyn, ed., *Apologia of Robert Keayne*, p. 9; Joseph B. Felt, *The Ecclesiastical History of New England* (Boston, 1855-62), II, 98; Scholz, " 'The Reverend Elders,' " pp. 131 ff.

tells us little of the interrelationship of the two drives, and it ignores an interrelationship of both with the theological concerns of the preachers.

The Puritan and ministerial drives were independent and interacting at the same time, a fact to be kept in mind. This has already been evidenced in passing. Roger Williams was Puritanism personified—so enmeshed himself, and seeking to such a degree to enmesh others, in the personal Christian quest as to ignore altogether the institutionalization of the quest. Yet his very Puritanism forced the fellowship to recognize itself as an institution when his antagonists among the ministers framed the "Model of Church and Civil Power" to rationalize their and the state's actions against him. The interrelationship is evidenced again when lay ardor such as that in Dorchester led the ministers to formalize their corporate control over the formation of new churches—excessive ardor provoked by the reverend elders *qua* preachers provoking an institutional limitation of ardor by the selfsame elders *qua* ministers. And the interrelationship—together with that of both ministerial and Puritan drives with theology—is evidenced even more sharply with respect to the concept of "visible saints."

Recall our earlier discussion of the covenanted gatherings of the godly in England. The tradition of such gatherings underlay the first churches in New England, the single exception being the church initially organized in Dorchester in 1630 and removing to Connecticut in 1635. Dorchester seemingly reflected its ministerial leaders and particularly Master John Warham who, in 1630, argued against the gatherings and for churches composed of "a mixed people,—godly, and openly ungodly."[15] As we have seen, there was a tendency even in England to idealize the gathering of the godly as the proper visible church vis-à-vis the invisible church of God's elect. But what constituted the prerequisites for membership in such a gathering in old England and at first in New? Very clearly

---

[15] "Governor Bradford's Letter Book," p. 75.

the requirement encompassed only a right knowledge of Christian doctrine, as expressed in a profession of faith, and right demeanor. There was, as Edmund S. Morgan has shown, no thought that the gathered godly were truly God's saints—although hopefully they were—or that the gathering, construed as a visible church, had any more than a very rough relationship to the invisible church.[16]

In England a concern for the gatherings was a ministerial or institutional concern, one of the few real, as against theoretic, institutional concerns allowed the ministers of the fellowship. Emanating from their Puritanism—and far more significant to them while in England—was the ministers' concern for the dialectic of God's relationship to man and the morphology of conversion. Again, recall the fundamentals.

The morphology of conversion embraced the necessity of man's preparing himself to receive the fruits of God's election, and to search for assurance of the fulfillment by salvation of that election.[17] We can consider these processes as two of three segments which make up the life of a man born and predestined to salvation—the first of the three being the life of sin antecedent to the onset of preparation—and we can visualize this life as a straight line with birth as the beginning and death as the end:

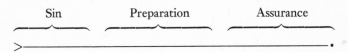

The segments of preparation and assurance can be further subdivided by points representing a progression of steps through which the predestined pass. Ten such steps were generally postulated, the first four most often as points of preparation, the last six of assurance.

---

16 In his *Visible Saints*.

17 See Perry Miller, " 'Preparation for Salvation' in Seventeenth-Century New England," in his *Nature's Nation* (Cambridge, Mass., 1967); Pettit, *Heart Prepared*, pp. 86 ff.; Morgan, *Visible Saints*, pp. 67 ff.

1. Attendance upon the Word.
2. Submission to the moral law (the Commandments).
3. Awareness of one's sins.
4. Fear of the consequence of sin.
5. Consideration of the promises of salvation propounded and published in the Bible.
6. A spark of faith, a will and desire to believe.
7. Doubt and despair of salvation.
8. Doubt, but also a feeling of assurance and a persuasion of mercy.
9. A grief for sin because it is sin (not because of its consequences).
10. Grace to endeavor to obey God's commandments.

Our visualization of the saint's life is, therefore, somewhat more complex. It constitutes, in effect, a scale:

Scale I

Sin	Preparation				Assurance				
	1	2	3	4	5	6	7	8	9	10

Note well, however, that this scale merely describes a man's visible condition. The stages reflected on the scale were arrived at experientially, that is to say, by virtue of the acts and emotions felt by men who ultimately arrived at a feeling of assurance and subsequently constructed the scale—primarily ministers. However subjective, and they were highly subjective, the stages were capable of finite examination, and one who was versed in their examination could think to discern them in himself and others.

With regard to the dialectical progression which describes God's actions upon men, recall the five basic concepts: election, vocation, justification, sanctification, and glorification. Omitting election and glorification—the first, by definition, before the beginning of time, the second after its end—we can visualize vocation (God's call), justification (God's imputation of Christ's righteousness), and sanctification (the effect of that

4 9970

imputation) as fixed points "V," "J," and "S" in the straight line of a saint's life. Again we have constructed a scale:

Scale II

V   J   S

>—————————————————————— .

Quite obviously our two scales describe the same thing, the life of one of God's saints. But each describes that life from a different vantage point. The second describes the saint's life from the vantage point of God, in effect describing God's actions upon the regenerate man. It is absolute. Glorification emanates from election, sanctification from justification, justification from vocation, and vocation is predetermined by election. And it is definitive. Once the process starts with election, it must end with glorification. The first scale, on the other hand, describes the saint's life from the vantage point of man by describing the saint's reaction to God's action upon him. A man upon whom God is acting according to Scale II reacts according to Scale I. Does it therefore follow that *any* man reacting according to Scale I is being acted upon according to Scale II? Absolutely? No! That was generally agreed. The stages on Scale I are too easily mistaken to make such a statement; they can even be feigned by hypocrites. We must be content with the proposition that all of the elect react according to Scale I, but not all who react according to that scale are of the elect. But if we are intent on discovering who among men are to be saved, or if we ourselves are to be saved, how are we to proceed?

In England this problem of how to proceed to apply what we have summed up in our scales to the determination of the elect was merely debatable, hence moot. It was framed in terms of the quest for assurance and was vital to the minister in his pastoral role and to the individual parishioner seeking some knowledge of his status with the Lord. But it had little institutional standing. Little in the everyday world depended upon the answer. In New England, however, the individual's status became a matter of institutional concern, and the prob-

Lincoln Christian College

lem was framed in terms of the correlation of the invisible and visible churches, of church membership, of institutions. For the ministers, as they arrived, were immediately involved in establishing more finite criteria for admission to the churches than the initial vague profession of faith and right demeanor. By 1635 they were demanding that, in addition to displaying Christian knowledge and conduct, "such as were to join" the churches should "declare what work of grace the Lord hath wrought in them."[18] In other words, the prospective member was being asked to apply the scales to himself and declare what it was in his life which he could point to as an indication of grace, and both be assured himself that he was one of the elect—a discernible or visible saint—and assure his neighbors.

This shift from the gathering of the merely godly to the gathering of the visible saints was a logical derivative of abstract English considerations of the nature of the church, the tradition of the gatherings, and covenant theology. The saints were in covenant with God. The gatherings, covenanted bodies of questing Christians, could be construed as the essential church. How easily could the two covenants be equated—the covenanted gathering becoming the product of the covenant with God? Master William Ames had expressed the notion in the abstract long before the fact in New England. The true church, he wrote, "is not firstly actually a Church, and afterward made partaker of Union and Communion with Christ; but because it is united to Christ, therefore it is the Church of Christ."[19] But logical as it might be, the shift precipitated a lengthy and complex theological debate among the ministers. On the question of the application of the scales, far more than on any other, they found their doctrines at variance.

The easiest course by far was simply to confine oneself to the elaborate morphology of conversion developed in England —that scale describing man's reaction to God's actions—and

---

[18] Hosmer, ed., *Winthrop's Journal*, I, 173.
[19] *The Workes of the Reverend and Faithful Minister of Christ William Ames* (London, 1643), II, 135.

leave God's actions upon man the mysteries they most properly were. Thus Master Thomas Hooker accepted in the abstract the logic of building his church upon the basis of visible sanctity, yet, in effect, denied the possibility of any adequate procedure by which to identify God's elect from the mass of men and was prone to deal in "charity" with the prospective member. To him the prospect's profession of God's grace could be little more than "a reason of his hope towards God," and Hooker would cast "the cause, with judicious charity, to hope and believe there is something of God and grace in the soul" making the prospect "fit for church society."[20] In terms of our scales, Hooker would utilize only Scale I (man's reaction to God's action) and would place the criteria for membership in the churches low, in the preparatory period, merely hoping and praying that he had caught God's saints in the church and held the number of hypocrites down.

Master Thomas Shepard, too, accepted the logic of a church of saints. But he would identify the elect in terms of a *perfect* adhesion to Scale I. For him that scale constituted a set of "rules" ordained by God (he seems to have forgotten that they were experientially derived by mere men) which the saints must follow on their way to glory. And he would build his church out of those men who, outwardly living according to the rules, were more than likely of the elect, for if all of the elect reacted to God's actions according to the rules, the more perfect the adhesion to the rules the greater the probability of election. "Bring men unto rules, and try men's estates by that," he wrote.[21]

To John Cotton, however, the morphology of conversion (Scale I) was always suspect. He could never forget that it was based upon man, not God, and that while it was true that the saint's life progressed through its stages, so too could the life of the unregenerate. Men must live according to the first scale insofar as they were able, but they must find evidence

---

[20] Quoted in Pettit, *Heart Prepared*, pp. 91, 100.
[21] Quoted in *ibid.*, p. 109.

of their sainthood in terms of the second. For him the crucial
point was faith (point six on Scale I). Was a man's faith born
of true justification or not? To put it another way: Did faith,
as a point on Scale I, equate with "J" on Scale II? Shepard
would answer that faith in the context of the entire Scale I—
of his "rules"—could be accepted as true faith. But for Cotton
this was to gauge faith by men's appearance or works, by apparent sanctification, and hazard a fundamental error—that
sanctification in some fashion preceded justification (reversing
the order of Scale II), even that works (living according to
Scale I) were a cause and not merely a derivative of God's
action. (Hooker, particularly, was open to this last charge
with his accent on the "easing preparation in a Christian soul
before his [union] with Christ.")[22] Living according to Scale
I was, to Cotton, only an outward indication of a possible inward condition, an apparent "seal" of God's grace. To be
safe a man must find a second, an inward seal, a justification
in terms of Scale II which underlay the faith discerned according to Scale I, validating that faith and the whole of a
life lived by Shepard's "rules." And Shepard's position was,
to Cotton, to hazard Christian sloth. A man finding assurance
in terms of outward appearance and being accepted within a
church of saints on that basis was likely to rest easy. Cotton
would not have this. In another work, using quotations and
paraphrases, I have summarized his position:[23]

> 'It is the desire of my heart by the grace of Christ,' he wrote,
> 'to provoke Christians (in this country of universal profes-
> sion) not to rest in any changes of graces, duties or ordinances
> (as church-fellowship etc.).' 'I would not wish Christians to
> build the signs of their Adoption [by Christ] upon any sanc-
> tification, but such as floweth from faith in Christ Jesus; for
> all other holiness, and righteousness . . . may be . . . mortal
> seed, and fall short of perseverance: whereas the least seed of

---

[22] "3 propositions which have divided Mr. Hooker and Mr. Cotton, in
New England," October 7, 1637, Colonial Office Papers, 1/9, 159, Public
Record Office, London, on microfilm in the Library of Congress, Washington, D.C.
[23] *Winthrop's Boston*, pp. 116-17.

THE FELLOWSHIP IN THE WILDERNESS 105

faith, and of that holiness which floweth from it abideth for
ever.' Take comfort in the true ordinances of the church, but
'while you enjoy them, trust not in them, nor think not to
stand upon this, that you are blessed in regard to them.' Take
comfort, too, in the Word and in following its commandments, but do not let it close your eyes to the nearness of God
Himself, 'for it is not all the *promises* in Scripture, that have
at any time wrought any gracious changes in any soul, or are
able to beget the faith of *God's Elect.*' Only true faith—faith
emanating directly from God, faith in the absolute perfection
of God's will and the utter desirability of 'closing' with God,
faith that leads one to say 'here I am as you have created me,
weak, abject, yearning for your comfort yet comforted only
as it befits your will'—only such faith is 'the Witness of the
Spirit itself, as it is distinguished from our Spirit.'

We need not delve deeply into the debates which these
positions precipitated. They were bitter. The differences between Hooker and Cotton undoubtedly played a part in the
former's departure with his people for Connecticut in 1636.
And they were lengthy. Shepard and Cotton began putting
their positions into writing in late 1635, and between Decem-
ber, 1636, and mid-1637 Cotton and his critics confronted each
other in a series of meetings as the fellowship resorted to their
ministerial meetings to attempt a resolution of the issues raised
by the differences. In the end the debate came down to this:
The vast majority of the ministers stood by the morphology
of conversion—Scale I. To Cotton, Scale II was not only more
important, but applicable. His fellow ministers were relying
on apparent sanctification alone, and while such sanctification
inevitably followed justification, it was not infallible evidence
of it. He would have men catch "sight of some work in [the]
soul as no hypocrite could attain unto," viz., a justifying faith
antecedent to sanctification and emanating from the Holy
Spirit itself.[24]

---

[24] Hosmer, ed., *Winthrop's Journal*, I, 217. Many of the pertinent materials of the ministerial dispute—both printed and manuscript—have been
brought together by Hall, ed., *Antinomian Controversy*, pp. 24-151,
173-98.

We ought, however, to realize that in the debates the majority of the ministers were far more institutional-minded than Cotton; their morphology *was* a more viable gauge by which to test prospective church members, and they knew it. Cotton, on the other hand, was the better Puritan, if by that we mean one who drives men to a direct confrontation with God. He was not another Williams, certainly, although at times his language resembled that of the *enfant terrible*—he once referred to a series of questions directed to him by the majority as so many "interrogatories" and likened himself to Christ confronted by the "High Priests"[25]—and on more than one occasion he thought to resolve the differences by removing from Massachusetts.

We must realize, too, that Cotton's Puritanism provoked the excesses of the antinomians. If he would not have his people rest in "any changes of graces, duties or ordinances," if he would have them "build the signs of their Adoption" upon no other sanctification but that which flowed "from faith in Christ Jesus," his people responded in kind: "I seek not for graces, but for Christ, I seek not for promises, but for Christ, I seek not for sanctification, but for Christ, tell me not of meditation and duties, but tell me of Christ."[26]

And we must realize, finally, that it was the excesses of Cotton's Boston followers which brought Cotton around and ended the ministerial debates. In Cotton the institutional and Puritan drives were in tenuous balance, and when the crisis came—when his followers rejected the morphology of conversion entirely and put their hopes on the Holy Spirit alone, on a mystical merger of man and God, on faith without works, on justification without sanctification—he reluctantly abandoned them and an element of his Puritanism for the safety of an institutional church. So abandoned, his followers were rapidly brought to heel. The Synod of 1637 condemned their eighty-two errors and eleven unsafe speeches; Anne Hutchin-

---

[25] Hall, ed., *Antinomian Controversy*, p. 46.
[26] *Ibid.*, p. 246.

son herself was tried by Cotton's own church in Boston and excommunicated, and (with others) she was tried by the civil authorities and banished from the commonwealth. The Holy Spirit unleashed was too dangerous a phenomenon even for Cotton, and to a former follower, then in exile in Rhode Island, he wrote: "I know not how you can build up either church or commonwealth but as an house without a foundation."[27]

The Triumph of the Ministerial Commitment

An excessive and disruptive religiosity emanating from Cotton as a preacher—a Puritan—was tried and banished from Massachusetts Bay in 1637. Religiosity within the limits of institutional and ministerial propriety won the day. And in the aftermath of the disturbances, the ministers set about firming up the foundations of their religious house.

Within the separate congregations there was a strong assertion of ministerial authority. Shepherds of the flock and academicians of the Lord the ministers had always considered themselves to be. Such was part of their ministerial upbringing. Master John Preston had defined his preaching as "a public interpretation or dividing the Word, performed by an ambassador or minister who speaks to the people instead of God." Master Richard Greenham urged at one time that lay discussions of religious matters, even personal meditations, "be of those things [only] which we heard of our ministers." And when the Plymouth settlers (then without a minister) wrote to their ministerial mentor in the 1620s asking if a mere layman serving as a ruling elder within the church could baptize and offer communion, the answer was an emphatic "no"; only the clergy, "the elders that teach and exhort and labor in the word and doctrine to which the sacraments are annexed" could administer such. Subsequently he wrote cautioning against

---

[27] [John Cotton] to "Beloved Brother" at Aquidneck, June 4, [1638], Cotton Papers, Prince Collection, Boston Public Library, Boston.

settling in the ministry any but a learned university man.[28] But in the hyperreligious aura of the 1630s in New England, errant congregations had stood against their ministers, the antinomians above all others, questioning and heckling the ministers with whom they disagreed. Now the ministerial offices—pastor and teacher—were put forward as divine, subordinating the almost equalitarian congregationalism of the 1630s. Church members must "yield obedience to their Overseers, in whatsoever they see and hear by them commanded to them from the Lord," for while the congregations choose the ministerial officer, "the office itself is ordained immediately by Christ, and the rule annexed to the office is limited by Christ only." "A truth of the Gospel taught by a Minister of the Gospel . . . bindeth to faith and obedience, not only because it is Gospel, but also because it is taught by a minister."[29]

Among the ministers themselves there was a strengthening of the fellowship. It had weathered a division on fundamentals, one provoked by its Puritanism, and the forms of its union were the more established by that fact—synods, councils, and the all-important private meetings of the reverend elders. What was clear (at least for the moment) was that none should enter into delicate questions without consultation and advice from the whole body of ministers. The lesson was not lost on Cotton. In 1639 he turned aside a question raised by his congregation on a certain Sabbath; during the following week he met with "all the Divines" and subsequently imparted to the congregation the fruits of this joint delibera-

---

[28] Gordon Stevens Wakefield, *Puritan Devotion: Its Place in the Development of Christian Piety* (London, 1957), p. 22; Emerson, ed., *English Puritanism*, p. 45; George D. Langdon, Jr., *Plymouth Colony: A History of New Plymouth, 1620-1691* (New Haven, 1966), p. 117. See also Haller, *Rise of Puritanism*, p. 172, where he argues that the preachers "went to press" in part to keep their religious control intact, publishing pamphlets and tracts specifically designed to guide the laity along the right lines. For a further discussion see Marc L. Schwarz, "The Religious Thought of the Protestant Laity in England, 1590-1640" (unpublished Ph.D. dissertation, University of California at Los Angeles, 1965).

[29] Rutman, *Winthrop's Boston*, pp. 129, 134.

tion.[30] Major works emanating from early New England were all collaborations to a greater or lesser extent—in some cases outright collaborations with authorship by "the Elders of the Several Churches in New-England" stipulated in the title, in others the reverend elders assigning the volume to be written to a particular minister best versed in the subject, in still others the volume being written independently by a single minister in regular consultation with the others.[31] And every such work proclaimed the essential unity of New England. "Satan hath been oft busy to make breaches among us," one ministerial pamphlet proclaimed. "Yet the ministers of Christ have been hitherto generally (if not all) of one heart and mind in the main and principal things of his Kingdom amongst us." "They never yet met, but grace hath overwrested corruption; peace, trouble; and truth, error, and so have most sweetly accorded in one."[32]

Firming up the foundations of the religious house was, however, but one aspect of the ministerial reaction to the excessive religiosity of the 1630s. There was a conjunctive shift of emphasis.

From the moment when the fellowship, in New England, accepted the logic of equating the saints in covenant with God with the godly gathered in covenant with one another, it had been enmeshed in the problem of identifying the saints. That problem—involving "celestial politics," as one writer has com-

---

[30] Keayne's Journal of John Cotton's American Sermons, 1639-1642, Massachusetts Historical Society, [p. 18].

[31] See, e.g., the correspondence in Cotton Papers, Prince Collection, Boston Public Library, between Peter Bulkeley and Cotton regarding the former's The Gospel-Covenant (London, 1646), between Thomas Shepard and Cotton regarding Shepard's Theses Sabbaticae (London, 1649), and the preface to Thomas Hooker's A Survey of the Summe of Church Discipline (London, 1648), in which he writes with reference to "all the Elders upon the [Connecticut] river, of New Haven, Guilford, Milford, Stratford, Fairfield and most of the Elders of the Churches in the Bay": "At a common meeting I was desired by them all, to publish what now I do."

[32] John Allin and Thomas Shepard, A Defence of the Answer unto the Nine Questions . . . (London, 1648), p. 29.

mented[33]—was never really resolved. When Cotton abandoned his followers, he did not immediately abandon his ideas, nor did his fellow ministers insist that he do so. The problem which the fellowship had debated so assiduously was simply dismissed by declaring the crucial issue unimportant. To paraphrase Cotton: All of the ministers concurred in holding that the churches should be composed of visible saints united in Christ, but the fact that some conceived of visibility in terms of the union itself (as he did) while others conceived of it in terms of man's reaction to the union (as the majority did) was a matter of indifference.[34]

More importantly, however, the fellowship tended to dismiss the problem by again separating the two covenants. It was a necessary expedient, a way to build a church upon a firm foundation, as visible sanctity—the criteria for which they had declared to be a matter of indifference—was not. Hence, where in the 1630s they had been inclined to say that it was God's "Covenant of Grace, which give the first Being to a church," they tended now to make the covenant among men the essential element and leave God's covenant out of it. Cotton: The "mutual covenant one with another . . . gives the first being to a church," for "that which doth not give them jurisdiction or power over one another, makes them not a Church by divine right." Master Richard Mather: "There is nothing else without this joining in Covenant, that can sufficiently distinguish [church members]; it is not Faith and Grace in their hearts, for some men are members of the visible church, and yet have no Grace, and others may have Grace and yet be no members and therefore this is not the thing that doth distinguish them." Master John Norton: There is a "distinction between the Covenant of Grace and the church cov-

---

[33] Scholz in " 'The Reverend Elders.' "

[34] Cotton, *The Way of Congregational Churches Cleared*, p. 54; *idem, The Covenant of Grace* (London, 1655), p. 59. The fellowship was resorting to an old distinction, valuable for its pragmatic uses: that between necessary and immutable things and *adiaphora*, things indifferent. See Dickens, *English Reformation*, pp. 78-79.

enant." "He who is admitted to the external communion of the church professes the name of Christ, is separated from the world by external and covenanted holiness (the kind which is properly recognized by common sense and formally inheres in the church covenant itself) and is endowed with a knowledge of God, true religion, and a character of purity without scandal in his outward life," but "a person may be admitted into the communion of the external visible church who is not endowed with the real internal holiness of regeneration and with justifying faith in Christ."[35]

Indeed, so strong was the stress on the covenant as the foundation of an institutional church as against the covenanted relationship of saint to God that some ministers questioned the validity of maintaining the profession of grace (evidence of being in covenant with God) as a criterion for adherence to the covenant of the church. Thus Peter Bulkeley wondered musingly to George Phillips in 1638 "whether those only that are in covenant and do evidence a work of grace, are to be received to all ordinances?" It was, to him, "a very doubtful question." And in 1642 Master Thomas Allen wrote Cotton himself to suggest that a relation of regeneration was unnecessary "seeing there [is] no expressed example for it in scripture."[36] These were extreme views tentatively put forward in private, however. The semantics of a gathering of visible saints was retained. The formalities by which men and women sought and gained admission to the churches were not changed; candidates were still tested for right knowledge, right conduct, and experienced grace—albeit the test and weighting of

---

[35] "Conference of the Elders of Massachusetts with the Rev. Robert Lenthall, of Weymouth, Held at Dorchester, Feb. 10, 1639," *Congregational Quarterly*, XIX (1877), 236-39; [Richard Mather], *Church-Government and Church-Covenant Discussed* (London, 1643), pp. 24-25; John Norton, *The Answer to the Whole Set of Questions of the Celebrated Mr. William Appolonius*, Douglas Horton, trans. (Cambridge, Mass., 1958), p. 26.

[36] Bulkeley to Phillips, n.d. but *ca.* 1642, Houghton Library, Harvard University, Cambridge, Mass.; Allen to Cotton, November 24, 1642, Hutchinson Collection, Massachusetts Archives, Boston.

experienced grace varied. Cotton, in the Boston church, continued to apply a rigid test for experienced grace, while more generally the ministers applied a rigid test of conduct and right knowledge but accepted the profession of grace "weakly" and "briefly done."[37] And the covenants to which the successful candidates adhered continued to declare, either implicitly or explicitly, that here were gatherings of the proven saints.

THE IRONY OF THE TRIUMPH

An aura of unity descended on "orthodox" New England—Massachusetts Bay, the Connecticut River towns, newly settled New Haven, Plymouth—in the aftermath of the antinomian disturbances, one exemplified in the phrase "one heart and mind in the main and principal things" previously quoted. Neither the phrase nor the aura should delude us, however. Orthodox New England possessed the semblance but not the substance of unity. Delicate questions were still asked among the ministers and disparity of doctrine and even practice was the rule, not the exception. The existence, side by side, of substantive disparity and the semblance of unity must be well understood. The latter was a response to the assumption that unity was an absolute good and was reflected in the institutionalized fellowship; the former was inherent in a movement which denied all authority but God's, and it could be encompassed within the fellowship only by regular resort to that device first utilized in New England in reconciling Cotton to his fellow ministers, that is, to declare *any* irreconcilable difference, *adiaphoron*—a thing indifferent.

And yet, even as Cotton made his peace in the 1630s, there was, so to speak, waiting in the wings, a difference so basic as to defy all efforts to resolve it or even to declare it indifferent.

---

[37] "A relation in what manner any persons are received into the congregations of New England, [1637]," Colonial Office Papers, 1/9, 166, Public Record Office. See also Robert A. Rees's brief survey, "Seeds of Enlightenment: Public Testimony in the New England Congregational Churches, 1630-1750," *Early American Literature*, III (1968), 22-29.

The crux of the theological debate of the 1630s had been the criteria by which to judge visible sainthood. But what of the very concept of a church of visible saints itself? That Hooker, in far-off Connecticut, should deal so charitably with the profession of grace and Shepard, at Cambridge, should test grace in terms of outward adherence to "the rules"; that Hooker, Shepard, and the majority of the ministers should react unfavorably to Cotton's excursion into celestial politics (however logical that excursion was); that in the aftermath of the lay excesses provoked by Cotton the tendency would be to separate the two covenants, provoking a questioning of whether a test of grace should remain a part of the qualification for church membership—all these reflected the enormous pressure placed upon the ministers' Puritanism by the whole concept of visible saints.

One need only ask a simple question to discern the nature of the pressure: What possibly can be the purpose of a church of saints and its sacraments—baptism and communion? We have noted in England the faint beginnings of a logical answer: to seal sainthood, to mark as completed a process of bringing man and God together which, given the theological dialectic, the progression linking election and glorification, begins and ends outside the church. Such an answer squared well with the institutional drive of the ministers. Their church would be in near-perfect concord with God's church (always providing, of course, that they could agree as to how the saints were to be discerned). But it squared not at all with their Puritanism. True, they could supply themselves with a role in the dialectic: God worked his wonder of calling men to an awareness of their elect estate most often through the voice of a minister. But the institution itself—the church of saints— had no evangelical function, no role in bringing men to the Christian quest. Ardent evangelism was the mark of their Puritanism, but a church of saints was not evangelical. Their church was, consequently, without purpose in the main work in which the preachers felt themselves most properly involved.

This was, indeed, high irony—the Puritanism of the preachers being betrayed by the very institution which the preachers as ministers created! In the years after 1640 some would seek to escape the trap, for the evangelical thrust did not die. Their efforts, however, were related to the society at large, to the psychosocial setting in which laymen received their preaching. It is to that which we must turn.

PREACHERS AND LAYMEN:
THE PSYCHOSOCIAL RECEPTION OF A RELIGIOUS GIFT

We have seen something of the impact of the preachers' social message upon laymen in old England and New. But what of the impact upon laymen of the preachers' religious message, and how did it affect events and developments in New England? More specifically, what was the context in which laymen received and acted upon the preachers' call for conversion from a life of sin to a life of Christian quest? The key word is conversion, for the simple fact is that lay Puritans—by definition laymen closely associated with the preachers and receiving by virtue of that association the gift of Puritanism —inevitably underwent a conversion experience. Indeed, historian Alan Simpson has gone so far as to say that the only thing all Puritans shared was the experience of conversion, "a new birth, which brings with it a conviction of salvation and a dedication to warfare against sin."[38] The preachers understood and urged this "new birth" in theological terms. Laymen, too, understood conversion theologically, albeit at times in a rough-and-ready fashion, as when Winthrop spoke of Christ taking possession of the soul and gathering together the bones of perfect "old man Adam." But unless we are prepared to accept as true the article of faith underlying the theological

---

[38] Simpson, *Puritanism in Old and New England*, p. 2. As most historians do, Simpson eschews explanation of conversion and settles for mere description. "There is no difficulty in discovering what this experience involved," he writes by way of preface to a description of the conversion of Thomas Goodwin as Master Goodwin himself described it.

explanation—that conversion was a response in men to an act of God—we must seek another basis for understanding. The search sends us to psychiatry, the metaphysics of the twentieth century.

Let us consider, for a moment, man as he totters from infancy toward death, his mind forever associating and rationalizing what is in it with what is entering it. At frequent points the disparity between what is already understood and what must be understood produces psychological punctuation marks —"crises," if by that term one does *not* inevitably intend to convey impending catastrophe. One such crisis is that continuous one by which the individual identifies himself in terms of the world about him—continuous because, as psychiatrist Erik H. Erikson writes, "the process 'begins' somewhere in the first true 'meeting' of mother and baby as two persons who can touch and recognize each other, and it does not 'end' until a man's power of mutual affirmation wanes."[39] The crisis peaks, however, at those points where the individual, having achieved one tentative identity in relationship to the social setting, is brought by a change of awareness or an actual change of setting to identify anew—the child, for example, secure within the social setting of the family, accommodating himself as a young man to an ever-wider world as he becomes aware of more and more of what is outside the family. Ultimately the broadening view of the child exceeds the world itself, and awareness is faced with the awesomeness of the minute self in an infinite universe. The child, even the toddler, might be taught religious precepts, but only with this last does the young man or woman truly come to grips with religion. Proferred theological systems, whatever they might encompass, offer an equating of self and universe by which the religious crisis is resolved. The "sense of incompleteness and imperfec-

[39] Erik H. Erikson, *Identity: Youth and Crisis* (New York, 1968), p. 23. See also Erikson's *Childhood and Society* (New York, 1950) and his application of theory to a historical figure: *Young Man Luther: A Study in Psychoanalysis and History* (New York, 1958), particularly pp. 254 ff.

tion; brooding, depression, morbid introspection and sense of
sin; anxiety about the hereafter; distress over doubts, and the
like"—symptoms of the religious crisis—give way to "a happy
relief and objectivity."[40]

The important phenomenon for us is that the process of
identification at any single moment involves both the internal
being and the external world. Erikson again: "Identity formation employs a process of simultaneous reflection and observa-
tion, a process taking place on all levels of mental functioning,
by which the individual judges himself in the light of what he
perceives to be the way in which others judge him in comparison to themselves . . .; while he judges their way of judg-
ing him in the light of how he perceives himself in comparison
to them." "We deal," therefore, "with a process 'located' *in
the core of the individual* and yet also *in the core of his communal culture*." "We cannot separate personal growth and
communal change, nor can we separate . . . the identity crisis
in individual life and contemporary crisis in historical development because the two help to define each other and are
truly relative to each other."[41]

For our purposes, too, we must note that identity formulation is, more often than not, a subconscious and automatic
process, a quiet and unspectacular adjustment of self and what
lies beyond self. Even at what has been discerned by psychiatry as the normative point of most extreme tension evoked
by the process—that as adolescence merges into young adulthood—the process entails an easy accommodation. The companion religious crisis, "incidental to the passage from the
child's small universe to the wider intellectual and spiritual
life of maturity," is easily and gently passed as well.[42] Identity
formulation can, however, become less easy as a result of inner

---

[40] William James, *The Varieties of Religious Experience: A Study in
Human Nature* (Modern Library ed.; New York, n.d.), p. 195. See also
E. D. Starbuck, *The Psychology of Religion* (London, 1901); Elmer T.
Clark, *The Psychology of Religious Awakening* (New York, 1929).

[41] *Identity*, pp. 22-23.

[42] James, *Varieties of Religious Experience*, p. 196.

conditions or outer circumstances. Indeed, it can reach toward catastrophic proportions. And as identity formulation becomes more difficult for an individual, he is "most susceptible to the propaganda of ideological systems which promise a new world-perspective at the price of total and cruel repudiation of an old one."[43] Religion in a religious age—the doctrine of conversion as our preachers preached it—can be construed as just such an ideology.

Such considerations cut across our study at a number of points. Winthrop was at the psychologically right age when he was set on the Christian quest by Master Culverwell—a young man of about eighteen. Can we interpret the event in terms of the resolution of an identity crisis and its "incidental" religious crisis, the problem of identity aggravated by a perceived contrast between a childhood identity within the quiet, stable confines of a gentry household and an outside world discerned as confused, changing, in flux? In other words, was the psychosocial setting such as to bring on Winthrop's conversion—conversion being simply the taking hold of and making personal the religious "ideology" proferred by Culverwell? Psychiatry would tend to say yes. Beyond the single case, can we postulate a social "species"[44] of which Winthrop was one, the whole existing in a similar psychosocial setting and prone to the same conversion experience? Historian Anthony Esler, succinctly summarizing the notion of "social generations" as developed by German, French, and Spanish scholars, would do so: "Men born about the same time," he writes, "exposed in their plastic early years to a common educational experience, and passing through the same span of history at the same rates of personal growth, will develop enough common ideas and attitudes to justify studying them as a distinct social group. Such a social generation in

---

[43] Erikson, *Young Man Luther*, p. 41.

[44] A better word would be "class" in the sense of simply a division or grouping; we eschew the word because of its connotations of socio-economic conflict.

fact comes to possess a group mind."[45] A group mind being merely the sum of its parts, and in this case each part undergoing a process of individual identity formulation, we can conceive of a generational identity process, the aggravation of that process to produce crisis, and the resolution in terms of a generational conversion. Obviously this line of thought cannot be carried too far. It does, however, suggest a relationship between an age-specific social milieu and conversion. A susceptibility to the conversion preached by the fellowship might well have been a natural phenomenon associated with gentry of roughly Winthrop's age and condition, or of small artisans and businessmen of the towns who felt threatened by new ways—to name two of the three groups we isolated in considering traditionalism.

The psychiatrist's considerations of identity cut across our exploration of American Puritanism at a second point as well. Keep in mind the fundamental points: The continuous process of identity formulation peaks at those times when the individual, by virtue of a change of awareness or an actual change of setting, is forced to identify anew; the difficulty of formulating anew is related to inner conditions and, more importantly for us, outer circumstances; difficulty brings susceptibility to ideology—in our case conversion. Surely the condition of emigration from old England to New, the departure from one social web and the necessity of encapsulating oneself in another, was such as to bring about an identity peak, to aggravate it, and to induce susceptibility to ideology. The ideology was ready to hand, proferred by those among the laymen who, like Winthrop, arrived heavy with God and with their English experience of conversion, and by the many ministers taking advantage of New England's "wide door of liberty" to preach so loudly their doctrine of conversion. Do we not have here ready explanation for that religious ardor, even revivalism, which appeared in New England in the initial years of settlement—the frenzy at Salem, in Dorchester, in Boston?

[45] Esler, *Aspiring Mind of the Elizabethan Younger Generation*, p. xi.

Yet if the question of identity underlay the religious ardor, we must immediately note that the resolution of the question was in process even while the settlements were convulsed by revivalism. In one sense resolution was being effected as men and women found their way into communal association, and all that we have said with respect to the reassertion within the towns of traditional values—unity, order, the family structure of society, diligence, and sublimation of self—has pertinence here. The arrival of families as strangers to the land and to each other, discomfited by the absence of a sense of unity in a common endeavor, aware of their values as felt-needs—all this is merely to cite particulars of a failure of identification. And that these same families sought satisfaction by coming together as a town, articulating a town covenant, and proceeding to build anew the traditional community of England is to cite particulars of a reforging of identity.

In another sense, however, identity was being resolved as men and women came together in the churches. We have noted religious ardor as a grasping at ideology and symptomatic of identity crisis, but we must quickly add that identity is not resolved in the heat of the moment when the individual takes hold of the ideology, but in the aftermath of that moment, when the individual locates himself with relationship to the value system which the ideology affirms. To put the point perhaps too simply: It is not in shouting, "Hosannah! I am saved," that our New Englander resolved his identity. He might well have shouted just that in the heat of coming to commitment to the ideology (although in all truth he would more than likely have shouted, "Lord! Lord! *Am* I saved?" and implicitly felt that by asking the question *sincerely* he had been answered affirmatively). Resolution came when he placed himself *among* the saved, when he had convinced himself, his friends, and his neighbors that he rightly sat with them as a member of the church, taking part with them in communion, in the baptism of his children, in the business of the meeting, and in the continuous moral inquisition which was the meeting's duty to itself and to the community. Resolution came, too, when he placed himself in terms of a negative group, when he felt himself *of* the church, hence occupying a definable position vis-à-vis those outside. Religious ardor as a symptom of identity crisis must therefore be followed in New England by a rush into church affiliation with its consequent resolution of crisis. And just such a rush has been shown to be the case in every modern study of the early New England communities.[46]

NEW ENGLAND APPLICATIONS

Looked upon in this fashion, several aspects of the Puritan and New England phenomena come into focus. We need not conceive of the thousands joining the New England churches in the 1630s as merely consummating their English Puritanism; indeed, no great portion of them was necessarily English Puritan at all in our sense of having been associated with the preachers in old England. Some surely were. But for those not, the exigencies of the psychosocial setting, together with the availability of the ideology, would induce ardor, a conversion experience, and cause them to solicit membership in the churches.

Moreover, while at the beginning of this chapter we wrote of the Holy Spirit being unleashed on men by the preachers as Puritans and institutionalized by the preachers as ministers, here we must add that the spirit would have been confined to an institution in any event. The doctrine of the preachers—ideology—might well lead abstractly to the notion of the "individual as a church in himself." But the psychosocial setting in which the doctrine was received—more particularly the inherent progression from crisis-evoked susceptibility to ideology to crisis-resolution within an institutional form of that

---

[46] See, e.g., Kenneth A. Lockridge, "The History of a Puritan Church, 1637-1736," *New England Quarterly*, XL (1967), 409; Darrett B. Rutman, "God's Bridge Falling Down: 'Another Approach' to New England Puritanism Assayed," *William and Mary Quarterly*, 3d ser., XIX (1962), 410.

ideology—barred the abstraction's way in real life. In old England there was an inherent tendency for the laymen associated with the preachers to look upon themselves as a definable group and, on the part of some, to institutionalize that feeling by entering the preachers' gatherings. In crisis-wracked New England there was an inherent tendency to resolve crisis within an institutionalized church. Even the antinomians, whose exaggeration of Cotton's teachings can be construed as an exaggeration of ideology in the throes of identity crisis, resolved that crisis within institutional frameworks erected in exile, although in the case of Anne Hutchinson herself the resolution came within the small bounds of her own family.

Most important with regard to the course of Puritanism in New England is the fact that identity was to an extent reformulated in a church defined according to the preachers' doctrine, and that at the peak of crisis—in the mid-1630s—that doctrine encompassed the notion of visible saints, one reflected institutionally in the requirement that would-be members prove not only their Christian knowledge and conduct but the work of God's grace within them—the first by a confession of faith, the second by subjecting themselves to the moral scrutiny of their neighbors, the third by a recounting of their conversion experience. The notion that the church among men could be constructed in such fashion as to be equatable to a degree with the invisible church of the elect was, as we saw, a fleeting doctrine among the ministers. They had no sooner put it forth than they were impaled upon its difficulties—difficulties which forced them to withdraw from the doctrine and concentrate upon the church as a body of men covenanted with each other rather than necessarily in covenant with the Lord. But while the ministers might withdraw from a hazardous doctrine, that doctrine had become a keystone of the new identity of those within the church. Their conversion, tested and approved by the community, had conferred a specific standing within the community and a special relationship to God. To question the identity they had achieved would be to precipitate crisis anew.

In a sense the preachers had created a monster which, if it did not devour them, curtailed their freedom of action. Abandoning celestial politics, they separated the two covenants in their theology—that between men to form a church and that between the saint and God. But they could not rewrite the church covenants to enunciate explicitly that, as even Cotton wrote, "many are truly called to the fellowship of the [church] Covenant . . . who were never elected nor approved . . . as heirs of salvation."[47] They could muse about the inappropriateness of requiring of would-be members a recounting of the conversion experience, as Master Thomas Allen did. But the threefold requirement for admission (the testing of knowledge, conduct, *and conversion*) had become ritualized as elements of self-identification and those identifying themselves in terms of the ritual could not easily countenance tampering. And the preachers would find their evangelicalism—the cardinal feature of their Puritanism—frustrated by the very nature of a church of saints. But any attempt to ease their frustrations was tempered by the nature of their congregations. Some could, as historian David Korbin has suggested, theologically redefine conversion. From an event testified to and sealed by church membership, they could interpret it as a long-term process completed under the aegis and through the instrument of the church.[48] Beyond this, they could not easily go. Attempts from the 1640s through the early 1660s to expand the jurisdiction of the church and bring within its purview children baptized in infancy but refraining from membership, the famed Halfway Covenant, brought with them storm and strife. The preachers of the fellowship themselves could not agree, either to the expansion of jurisdiction or to labeling the point an *adiaphoron* and letting each preacher and congregation do as it pleased, and their fragile fellowship was split by conten-

---

[47] Cotton, *The Grounds and Ends of the Baptisme of the Children of the Faithfull* (London, 1647), pp. 66-67.

[48] Korbin, "The Expansion of the Visible Church in New England: 1629-1650," *Church History*, XXXVI (1967), 189-207.

tion. Moreover, preachers favoring such an expansion found opposition within their congregations—opposition explainable in just such terms as we have used: The tampering with ritualized admission requirements even to this small extent challenged those already in the churches whose self-identity rested upon the ritual.[49] Indeed, New England's religious scene assumed a patchwork quality; disputes flared here and there—with this one element in common: Individual ministers, having arrived at objective truths regarding the nature of the church, sought to impose those truths within identity structures highly subjective to New England townsmen, the latter accepting or rejecting the truths of the ministers, coalescing into or dividing from churches, in terms of the identity structure of their particular town.

IN NEW ENGLAND, MERELY CHURCHES

At the beginning of this chapter, as we shifted from a consideration of traditionalism to a consideration of religion, we postulated that the religious course in New England involved four elements: the preachers' evangelicalism; the ministerial values of the preachers; the theological morphology of conversion; and the timeless nature of man. The first and third correlate easily, for the latter rationalized the former. So too do the first and fourth. The preachers had in early New England an audience prone, by virtue of an emigration-induced identity crisis, to accept their evangelical doctrine as ideology. And the second and fourth correlate, for if the ministerial values led toward institutionalization, so too did the necessity of resolving identity within the institutional expression of the ideology. But ministerial values and the necessity for men to identify

---

[49] Scholz, " 'The Reverend Elders,' " deals with the trials of the fellowship in this controversy; Robert G. Pope, "The Half-Way Covenant: Church Membership in the Holy Commonwealths, 1648-1690" (unpublished Ph.D. dissertation, Yale University, 1967) deals with the contention between preachers and congregations.

within the scope of an institution combined *against* the evangelical thrust. That path which we began as the fellowship formed so long before in England out of preachers ardent to take God's word to the people—that *Puritan* fellowship—has led merely to disparate churches, inherent in the identity structure of New England, but churches no longer qualified by the adjective *Puritan*, as we have defined that word.

EPILOGUE

New England has a history apart from Puritanism, but of which Puritanism was a part. In the preceding pages we have been concerned with the problem of defining Puritanism within a conceptual scheme useful as an analytical tool when applied to New England. And we have, in brief, defined Puritanism as an influence radiating from a Christian fellowship of evangelical preachers, having its specific effect (sometimes dominant, sometimes merely tangential) by virtue of its actions upon and interactions with other definable elements.

We could extend our consideration of action and interaction. Such broad subjects as "Puritan" law and "Puritan" literature, for example, demand consideration in terms of the action and interaction of the influence of the fellowship and the English legal traditions, of the fellowship and English literary forms and traditions.[1] More specifically: In passing we mentioned the covenant, but we have omitted an extended discourse on the covenant fixation as a continuing mark of New England—indeed, so firm a fixation was it that in eighteenth-century Connecticut a group formed themselves as an Anglican church by writing a covenant![2] But does not the fixation fit easily into the conceptualization we *have* outlined? The covenant can be linked to Puritanism in the sense that we find the notion in the fellowship; but it was also used to articulate a traditional form of village society when men and women felt the absence of traditional form. The covenant fixation, then, can be conceived as emanating from Puritanism *qua* the fellowship interacting with traditionalism as a felt-need evoked by the very nature of the settlement process.

---

[1] Harold S. Jantz, *The First Century of New England Verse* (Russell & Russell ed.; New York, 1962), and George Lee Haskins, *Law and Authority in Early Massachusetts: A Study in Tradition and Design* (New York, 1960), are suggestive along these lines. Similarly, Bernard Bailyn is suggestive on the interaction of the fellowship and traditonal mercantile notions in his *The New England Merchants in the Seventeenth Century* (Cambridge, Mass., 1955).

[2] I am grateful for this information to Bruce Steiner of Ohio University, whose research is deep in eighteenth-century Connecticut Anglicanism.

Consider, too, the morality and sense of sin so often commented upon in the New England character. Can it not be traced from the traditional English community, through an articulation and strengthening on the part of the preachers, to an identity-linked ritualization in New England—setting identity in terms of a moral boundary separating the acceptable from the nonacceptable?[3] Cannot the sense of mission, of the New Englanders being a favored people of God through whom great things would occur in the world, be traced from the interaction of the preaching of the fellowship and the necessities of identification—the latter an extrapolation from that comfortable sense of identity which the New Englander found within his church? Cannot the renewed Jeremiad, the bemoaning of the fallen state of the land—not England, this time, but New England—which began at roughly mid-century, be explained in terms of the fellowship and psychosocial considerations? Lamentations were within the English tradition of the fellowship, triggered anew in New England by the internal controversy over the Halfway Covenant, by the discernible fact that the preachers' freedom of action as evangelists and their privileges of action as ministers were curtailed by their congregations, and by what they conceived as their declining influence in the society. But the Jeremiad was also within the tradition of man—part of the ceremonial rededication of identity-imparting institutions which, as Erik Erikson notes, is necessary to the identity imparted.[4]

And finally, is not the true nature of the falling away from religion on the part of the New Englanders—that phenomenon bemoaned by the ministerial Jeremiahs in their lamentations of the degenerate conditions within the churches—implicit in our conceptualization? The exigencies of the settlement process brought on an identity crisis and a susceptibility to ideology. But as an identity structure was reformulated, both

---

[3] Sociologist Kai T. Erikson has moved in this direction in *Wayward Puritans: A Study in the Sociology of Deviance* (New York, 1966).
[4] Erikson, *Identity*, p. 224.

religiously in terms of the churches and secularly within the towns, particularly as the children of the first settlers grew to maturity within that structure and passed easily, without crisis, from youth to adulthood, identity became divorced from ideology. Where membership within a church involved nothing more than easy formality, men would still join; but to the degree that membership involved commitment to doctrine *qua* ideology, men tended to refrain.[5] Declining church membership relative to town populations was one result; the reduction of membership requirements to formalities was another. And as new generations structured their identity apart from ideology, even in some cases apart from churches, men tended to resent doctrine and any minister who sought to impose it upon them. Particularly was this the case in new towns, for it is a phenomenon of the latter half of the century that new communities were frequently without churches for a decade or more after settlement; in such towns a church was desired as traditional and necessary—but only as a *pro forma* social institution mirroring the town's identity structure. Evangelical ministers might attempt here and there to bring men back to ideology, as Solomon Stoddard did at century's end in North-ampton, Massachusetts, when he enunciated an explicit evangelical function for the church and opened membership to all of Christian deportment in the hope that within and by virtue of the church men could be brought to conversion. But not until well along in the eighteenth century, when the passage from youth to maturity was, in view of changed outer conditions, difficult and susceptibility to ideology great—not until such time do we see again the sort of religious fervor which we saw in the 1630s. So great a fervor was it then that historians have set it apart as "the great awakening," but it could just as easily be viewed as an extension of our own considerations. The functional relationship of parts which evoked the awakening—evangelical preachers and an audience prone to ac-

---

[5] Edmund S. Morgan, "New England Puritanism: Another Approach," *William and Mary Quarterly*, 3d ser., XVIII (1961), 236-42.

cept their message by virtue of an identity crisis—seems little different from that which evoked the first awakening of the 1630s.[6]

We could extend our considerations far, indeed! But our problem has been one of conceptualization, not exposition. If our conceptualization both of Puritanism and the nature of the historical process as sequential action and interaction of parts is valid, we have, in effect, constructed a paradigm to serve as the basis for near-unending exposition of what occurred and emerged in New England. And insofar as New England acted and interacted with other sections ultimately making up the United States, we have laid down, to some extent, a basis for American history.

---

[6] This would seem to be the direction of contemporary "Awakening" studies. See J. M. Bumsted's " 'What Must I Do To Be Saved?': A Consideration of Recent Writings on the Great Awakening in Colonial America," forthcoming in the Canadian Association of American Studies, *Bulletin*. Cf. Miller's "Introduction" in Miller and Johnson, comps., *The Puritans*, I, 3-4.

PURITAN STUDIES:
A SHORT BIBLIOGRAPHICAL ESSAY

For over three and a half centuries men have written about New England and its Puritanism. In the seventeenth century New England's ministerial and lay leaders wrote, driven by their belief that they were recording the hand of God at work. William Bradford wrote his truly beautiful *Of Plymouth Planation, 1620-1647;* John Winthrop his *Journal "History of New England,"* *1630-1649;* Edward Johnson his *Wonder-Working Providence of Sions Saviour in New England;* Cotton Mather his heavy-handed but rich *Magnalia Christi Americana; or, The Ecclesiastical History of New England.* (There are several editions of each, but the most readable are Samuel Eliot Morison's of Bradford [New York, 1953], James Kendall Hosmer's of Winthrop [2 vols.; New York, 1908], J. Franklin Jameson's of Johnson [New York, 1910], and the two-volume Hartford edition of Mather [1852-53].) Peter Gay's *A Loss of Mastery: Puritan Historians in Colonial America* (Berkeley and Los Angeles, 1966) is a good brief introduction to this initial historiography.

Providential history was not abandoned abruptly in the eighteenth century. Indeed, in a sense one can consider a continuing tradition of ecclesiastical history to be a collateral descendant. Joseph B. Felt, *Ecclesiastical History of New England* (2 vols.; Boston, 1855), Henry Martyn Dexter, *The Congregationalism of the Last Three Hundred Years* (New York, 1880), and Williston Walker's editing of *The Creeds and Platforms of Congregationalism* (New York, 1893) are prime examples. But such history was gradually supplanted by secular history. Not God's will but man's politics dominates Thomas Hutchinson's three-volume *History of the Colony and Province of Massachusetts Bay* (Boston, 1764-1828) —best used in Lawrence Shaw Mayo's Cambridge, Mass., 1936 edition. Man's politics in terms of the emergence of political liberty dominated John Gorham Palfrey's five-volume *A Compendious History of New England* (Boston, 1858-90). Early New England's negation of political liberty dominates Brooks Adams' *Emancipation of Massachusetts* (Boston and New York, 1887). And the place of New England's institutions in an evolutionary stream conceived as running from the Teutonic forests through Saxon England dominates Herbert Baxter Adams' *The Germanic Origin of New England Towns* (Baltimore, 1882).

The last two titles set the stage for a twofold approach to early New England which prevailed through the first decades of the twentieth century. On the one hand was a continuing assault which wrenched figures of the time out of context, threw words like "theocracy" around with abandon, and read nineteenth-century class struggles into the seventeenth century. The climax of the assault was James Truslow Adams' *The Founding of New England* (Boston, 1921) and the first volume of Vernon Louis Parrington's *Main Currents in American Thought*, which deals with *The Colonial Mind* (New York, 1927). The other approach was a less spectacular but more firmly based succession of institutional and "New England in the Empire" studies best represented by the pertinent parts of Herbert L. Osgood's *The American Colonies in the Seventeenth Century* (3 vols.; New York, 1904) and Charles M. Andrews' *The Colonial Period of American History* (4 vols.; New Haven, 1934-38).

The reaction to both approaches was soon forthcoming. Where Parrington made of Puritanism a thing deadening to the free mind of man, and Osgood and Andrews subsumed New Englanders to broad themes, Samuel Eliot Morison first depicted Puritans as men —this in his *Builders of the Bay Colony* (Boston and New York, 1930)—then attributed to them a first American enlightenment—in *The Puritan Pronaos: Studies in the Intellectual Life of New England in the Seventeenth Century* (New York, 1936) and his work on Harvard, notably *The Founding of Harvard College* (Cambridge, Mass., 1935). In this effort Morison drew in part upon the work of two scholars of early American literature, Thomas Goddard Wright, *Literary Culture in Early New England, 1620-1730* (New Haven, 1920), and Kenneth Murdock, *Increase Mather: The Foremost American Puritan* (Cambridge, Mass., 1925). And Wright and Murdock, not Morison—the litterateurs rather than the historian—were precursors of the giant to come.

The giant was Perry Miller, another litterateur. In one work after another he attacked the published works of the Puritans, seeking to piece together the structure of ideas which, in sum, would constitute a Puritan and New England mind. His road was not easy. Critics were skeptical of his early works. But *Orthodoxy in Massachusetts, 1630-1650* (Cambridge, Mass., 1933); *The Puritans* (New York, 1938), an anthology prepared in collaboration with Thomas H. Johnson; *The New England Mind: The Seventeenth Century* (New York, 1939); *Jonathan Edwards* (New York, 1949), together with the continuing studies of Murdock, most notably *Literature & Theology in Colonial New England* (Cambridge, Mass., 1949) did their work well. In the 1950s appeared Miller's *The New England Mind: From Colony to Province* (Cambridge, Mass., 1953), *Roger Williams: His Contribution to the American Tradition* (New York, 1953), and a collection of articles published as *Errand into the Wilderness* (Cambridge, Mass., 1958). By then he was not only accepted as the dominant figure in Puritan studies, but a generation of scholars had appeared committed to a Millerite approach to Puritan materials.

Miller died in 1963, his last book being a collection of essays published posthumously as *Nature's Nation* (Cambridge, Mass., 1967). During the past few years his work has been amended, most notably by Edmund S. Morgan in his *Visible Saints: The History of a Puritan Idea* (New York, 1963) and Norman Pettit, *The Heart Prepared: Grace and Conversion in Puritan Spiritual Life* (New Haven, 1966). But through the 1960s the Millerite generation has held sway. Intellectual history has been frankly exegesic, while historians of society, politics, economics and generally the affairs of men have molded their studies to the framework Miller erected. The synthesis has broadened our understanding considerably. A mere enumeration of titles is beyond the scope of this note, but major contributions come to mind: Edmund S. Morgan's *The Puritan Family: Religion and Domestic Relations in Seventeenth-Century New England* (Boston, 1944), his *The Puritan Dilemma: The Story of John Winthrop* (Boston, 1958), and most recently *Roger Williams: The Church and the State* (New York, 1967); Babette Levy, *Preaching in the First Half Century of New England History* (Hartford, 1945); Thomas Jefferson Wertenbaker, *The Puritan Oligarchy: The Founding of American Civilization* (New York, 1947); Alan Simpson, *Puritanism in Old and New England* (Chicago, 1955); Emil Oberholzer, Jr., *Delinquent Saints: Disciplinary Action in the Early Congregational Churches of Massachusetts* (New York, 1956); George Lee Haskins, *Law and Authority in Early Massachusetts: A Study in Tradition and Design* (New York, 1960); Larzer Ziff, *The Career of John Cotton: Puritanism and the American Experience* (Princeton, 1962); Richard S. Dunn, *Puritans and Yankees: The Winthrop Dynasty of New England, 1630-1717* (Princeton, 1962); George D. Langdon, Jr., *Pilgrim Colony: A History of New Plymouth, 1620-1691* (New Haven, 1966); Mary Jeanne Anderson Jones, *Congregational Commonwealth: Connecticut, 1636-1662* (Middletown, Conn., 1968); and Richard L. Bushman, *From Puritan to Yankee: Character and the Social Order in Connecticut, 1690-1765* (Cambridge, Mass., 1967).

If the synthesis has proven productive, it has for some proven constrictive. A number of trends outside of the relatively small realm of American Puritanism—even outside of history, in sociology, anthropology, and psychology—have combined to create a feeling of unease. Historians have become more concerned with the nature of their field, and such studies as Robert F. Berkhofer, Jr.'s *A Behavioral Approach to Historical Analysis* (New York, 1969) implicitly criticize simplistic conceptualizations of New England and its Puritanism, of the transit of culture from old England to New, and of the interplay of action and ideas. Historians have discovered in quantification and, in a few cases, the computer, tools with which they can cope with the enormous amount of discrete materials buried in town records and the like, and their broadened base of evidence is indicating a structure of life unencompassed by the Millerite framework. They have become aware of methodological tools in other disciplines through such works as Erik H. Erikson's *Young Man Luther: A Study in Psychoanalysis and History* (New York, 1958); his *Identity: Youth and Crisis* (New York, 1968); Kai T. Erikson's *Wayward Puritans: A Study in the Sociology of Deviance* (New York, 1966); Robert Redfield's *The Little Community: Viewpoints for the Study of a Human Whole* (Chicago, 1955); Conrad M. Arensberg and Solon T. Kimball's *Culture and Community* (New York, 1965); Eric R. Wolf's *Peasants* (New York, 1966). They have discerned trends in the historiography of English Puritanism, notably the tendency to consider Puritanism in terms of a peculiar ministry—the starting point for our consideration—first in William Haller's *The Rise of Puritanism* (New York, 1938) and most recently in H. C. Porter's *Reformation and Reaction in Tudor Cambridge* (Cambridge, 1958); Charles H. and Katherine George's *The Protestant Mind of the English Reformation, 1570-1640* (Princeton, 1961); John F. H. New, *Anglican and Puritan* (Palo Alto, Calif., 1964)—frequently described as a rebuttal to the Georges but more aptly termed an amendment; and Patrick Collinson, *The Elizabethan Puritan Movement* (Berkeley and Los Angeles, 1967). Such a ministerially-oriented Puritanism links easily to the religious scene of mid-seventeenth-century England as depicted by such as Geoffrey Nuttall, *Visible Saints: The Congregational Way, 1640-1660* (Oxford, 1957). But, unfortunately, a sophisticated link to the broad, lay Puritanism of the 1630s and 1640s which is the essence of the work of such as Christopher Hill (see particularly *Society and Puritanism in Pre-Revolutionary England* [New York, 1964]) and Michael Walzer (*The Revolution of the Saints* [Cambridge, Mass., 1965]) has yet to be developed.

Above all, however, younger scholars have become aware of the direction of French and English social history as it pertains to the pre-industrial world of the sixteenth, seventeenth, and eighteenth centuries. The bibliography in this area is already long, but the main thrusts are three in number. First, the exploration in depth of pre-industrial population and communities. See E. A. Wrigley, ed., *An Introduction to English Historical Demography from the Sixteenth to the Nineteenth Century* (New York, 1965) with its excellent bibliography; Peter Laslett, *The World we have lost* (New York, 1965); and the various essays in D. V. Glass and D. E. C. Eversley, eds., *Population in History: Essays in Historical Demography* (London, 1965), and *Daedalus* (Spring, 1968), an issue devoted to "Historical Population Studies." Second, the exploration of pre-industrial social groupings, exemplified best in Lawrence Stone's *The Crisis of the Aristocracy, 1558-1641* (Oxford, 1965) and his numerous articles, most notably "Social Mobility in England, 1500-1700," *Past & Present*, XXXIII (1966). Third, the exploration of the early-modern family, principally in the work of Philippe Ariès, *Centuries of Childhood: A Social History of Family Life*, Robert Baldick, trans. (New York, 1962). Such work is appropriate to early New England in terms of methodology. But its most striking aspect is its reduction of peculiarly Puritan traits of social and economic behavior to simply pre-industrial traits, and, more generally, its reduction of peculiarly American traits in the seventeenth and eighteenth centuries to simply Anglo-American traits.

The new directions have slowly exerted an influence on studies of New England. Anthony N. B. Garvan, as long ago as 1951, could not fit his work on the spatial relationships of the New England town into a Millerite framework, hence wrote his *Architecture and Town Planning in Colonial Connecticut* (New Haven) without reference to Puritanism. Others addressing themselves to architecture have been more direct, John Coolidge arguing in "Hingham Builds a Meetinghouse," *New England Quarterly*, XXXIV (1961), that New England's meetinghouses were international rather than peculiar in style. Recently Marian Card Donnelly, *The New England Meeting Houses of the Seventeenth Century* (Middletown, Conn., 1968) has ambiguously agreed. Bernard Bailyn in his *The New England Merchants in the Seventeenth Century* (Cambridge, Mass., 1955) posited the prevalence of traditional economic values as well as Puritan values. Emery Battis in his *Saints and Sectaries: Anne Hutchinson and the Antinomian Controversy in the Massachusetts Bay Colony* (Chapel Hill, N.C., 1962) utilized sociological and psychological methodology, although in not fully satisfactory fashion. Sumner Chilton Powell's *Puritan Village: The Formation of a New England Town* (Middletown, Conn., 1963) found the essence of Sudbury less in Puritanism and more in English tradition. In my own *Winthrop's Boston: Portrait of a Puritan Town, 1630-1649* (Chapel Hill, N.C., 1965) I attempted to depict the interaction of social parts—one of which was the church. The book led to a direct questioning of the prevalent framework in "The Mirror of Puritan Authority," originally published in George A. Billias, ed., *Law and Authority in Colonial America* (Barre, Mass., 1965). In the last few years the main thrust has been toward the demographic and social analysis of New England communities. Only articles have appeared thus far. Among the principal ones: Philip J. Greven, Jr., "Historical Demography and Colonial America," *William and Mary Quarterly*, 3d ser., XXIV (1967)—an excellent introduction to the whole approach; his "Family Structure in Seventeenth-Century Andover, Massachusetts," *ibid.*, XXIII (1966); his "Old Patterns in the New World: The Distribution of Land in Seventeenth Century Andover," *Essex Institute Historical Collections*, CI (1965); Kenneth A. Lockridge, "Land, Population and the Evolution of New England Society, 1630-1790," *Past & Present*, XXXIX (1968); his "The Population of Dedham, Massachusetts, 1636-1736," *Economic History Review*, 2d ser., XIX (1966); Lockridge and Alan Kreider, "The Evolution of Massachusetts Town Government, 1640 to 1740," *William and Mary Quarterly*, 3d ser., XXIII (1966); John Demos, "Families in Colonial Bristol, Rhode Island: An Exercise in Historical Demography," *ibid.*, XXV (1968); and his "Notes on Life in Plymouth Colony," *ibid.*, XXII (1965); James A. Henretta, "Economic Development and Social Structure in Colonial Boston," *ibid.*, XXII (1965); William I. Davisson, "Essex County Wealth Trends: Wealth and Economic Growth in 17th Century Massachusetts," *Essex Institute Historical Collections*, CIII (1967). But full studies—and additional articles—are not far behind.

Much of this newer work ignores Puritanism completely; some of it is pressed into the prevalent synthesis, straining both the new approaches and the old synthesis. In either case, the work is creating tensions in New England and Puritan studies, a fact clearly evidenced in Edmund S. Morgan's "The Historians of Early New England," in Ray Allen Billington, ed., *The Reinterpretation of Early American History* (San Marino, Calif., 1966). Perhaps by the present work—a calculated attempt to bridge old and new—the tension may be somewhat eased.

Whatever evolves out of this tension, one thing is clear. Far from the threshed-over field of dry stubble which Perry Miller was advised to eschew in the early 1930s, the field is filled today with threshers reaping a rich harvest. One sign of this is the steady appearance of Puritan materials in modern editions and anthologies; another is the number of collections of scholarly essays appearing. Among the most recent of the former are David D. Hall's *The Antinomian Controversy, 1636-1638: A Documentary History* (Middletown, Conn., 1968); Larzer Ziff's *John Cotton on the Churches of New England* (Cambridge, Mass., 1968); Edmund S. Morgan's *Puritan Political Ideas, 1558-1794* (Indianapolis, 1965) and his *The Diary of Michael Wigglesworth, 1653-1657* (New York, 1965); Bernard Bailyn's *The Apologia of Robert Keayne* (New York, 1964); Jeannine Hensley's *The Works of Anne Bradstreet* (Cambridge, Mass., 1967); A. W. Plumstead's *The Wall and the Garden: Selected Massachusetts Election Sermons, 1670-1775* (Minneapolis, 1968); and Everett H. Emerson's *English Puritanism from John Hooper to John Milton* (Durham, N.C., 1968). Among essay collections, one notes Sydney V. James' excellent *The New England Puritans* (New York, 1968); David D. Hall's comparable *Puritanism in Seventeenth-Century Massachusetts* (New York, 1968); and Michael McGiffert's *Puritanism and the American Experience* (Reading, Mass., 1969).

One segment of Puritan studies remains to be considered, albeit briefly—that in which the phenomenon of Puritanism is drawn as a convoluted but single strand through the whole of American history. The effort is truly impressive in the hands of such masters as Edmund S. Morgan—when he draws Puritanism into the American Revolution in "The Puritan Ethic and the American Revolution," *William and Mary Quarterly*, 3d ser., XXIV (1967); Sydney E. Ahlstrom, "The Puritan Ethic and the Spirit of American Democracy," in George L. Hunt, ed., *Calvinism and the Political Order* (Philadelphia, 1965); William G. McLoughlin, "Piety and the American Character," *American Quarterly*, XVII (1965); David W. Noble, *Historians Against History: The Frontier Thesis and the National Covenant in American Historical Writing* (Minneapolis, 1965); Chard Powers Smith, *Yankees and God* (New York, 1954); George M. Stephenson, *The Puritan Heritage* (New York, 1952); and Ralph Barton Perry, *Puritanism and Democracy* (New York, 1944). But the thrust of such works seems wrong. Puritanism on such a broad scale is whatever the authors conceive it to be, but when their work is rooted in the soil of seventeenth-century New England, they would seem to be obliged to come to grips with Puritanism as more than an ambiguity, as, indeed, the societal phenomenon in need of a definition which we have conceived it to be. And only when the root phenomenon is clearly delimited can its legacy be assessed.

Index